Practical guide
for
SHAMANIC RITUALS

Harmony Zen S.A.
Cours de Rive 16
Case Postal 3358
CH- 1211 Genève 3

© 2004, **Harmony Zen** Editions

Published with the autorization of "Éditions Exclusif"

I.S.B.N. : 2-88493-004-3

JOHN CREEK

Practical guide for SHAMANIC RITUALS

INTRODUCTION

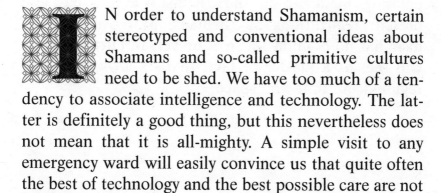N order to understand Shamanism, certain stereotyped and conventional ideas about Shamans and so-called primitive cultures need to be shed. We have too much of a tendency to associate intelligence and technology. The latter is definitely a good thing, but this nevertheless does not mean that it is all-mighty. A simple visit to any emergency ward will easily convince us that quite often the best of technology and the best possible care are not sufficient to save lives.

Certain ancient civilizations were highly sophisticated despite their lack of technology. For example, the Mayas who had never invented the wheel nevertheless built temples the architecture of which still remains a wonder and a mystery up until today. The same is true of ancient Egypt : How could we call primitive a people who left behind such pyramids ? As we begin to examine these civilizations, we observe that the term "primitive" does not have the same connotation anymore, and that the absence of technology and comforts which we enjoy in our modern world is not tantamount to a lack of intelligence; what we are up against is more of a different turn of mind. We all have much to gain by studying and preserving it in our own lives.

To understand Shamanism, we also need to open up our hearts and minds to new perspectives, to different ways of perceiving and confronting reality. For example, in the language of the Hopis, a Native American nation in the State of Arizona, there is no word for war. In the same area, another tribe, that of the Navajos, is famous for its healing rituals using paintings made out of sand. The list is long of past and present realizations by shamans. Moreover, shamanism has no boundaries: it is universal. Further on we will see, as a matter of fact, that its laws transcend regionalism, time and space.

Two Ways to Approach Shamanism

The first way to approach Shamanism is more traditional. The candidate must have undergone traumatic experiences which caused him to transform his perception of the world. These experiences litterally project him into the world of shamanism. He then learns rituals, methods of perceiving reality, traditional forms of meditation, and so on. After many years of practice, he will gradually start to understand why these techniques work. Sometimes also shamans from the old school perpetuate their know-how without any explanations. They do not need anything else. Their shamanic know-how is just as valid as that of others. The newcomer or candidate undergoes an initiation; he must follow the rules just as his predecessors have. This system, which has survived up until present times, has proved its value. But not for everyone.

The second way is more modern. It is a Western approach, for our time. The beginner gradually learns shamanism. He is slowly guided into this path, and he understands what is happening. There is no mystery in this method. It is a gradual awakening of the unique possibilities of each individual. The initiation process takes longer, because understanding each step is necessary before going any further.

As you can imagine there are as many people in favor of each of these two methods. The second one is easier to approach; it does not require any formal guide or master. It can take place at the candidate's own pace.

The ideal is to mix both. It is sometimes very interesting to share this type of experience with an initiate, with someone who can answer your questions. It is necessary to undergo ritual saunas (which we will describe further on) without the presence of a third party. You must judge for yourself whether or not it is important for you to have a teacher. Once again no one method is better than another, the choice is up to you.

The Method Offered in this Book

The method we offer in this book is based on a variety of shamanic traditions. It is mainly inspired from Native American and Hawaiian traditions which survived in our modern world. These traditions were adapted to suit the needs of urban civilization. Most of us live in cities, where we spend most of our existence. Shamanism is an art which has survived over thousands of years, and it continues to do so very well in the urban conditions of this century. This blend of continental and island cultures gives us a greater flexibility in our shamanic practice, as you will observe through your own experience.

We have also integrated certain practices taken from European wicca, practices from Asia and many other places in the world. Take what suits you, try out all possibilities and then keep what seems most adequate for your own personal needs. With time, you will even end up innovating and creating your own shamanic rituals. What matters is entering into contact with the spiritual world, changing your perception of the universe. We prefer a mellow, simple approach. This is what we offer.

The key to success mainly resides in the conviction that you can be successful in this path. Another important condition is to be truly and keenly interested by the subject. Our goal, in writing this book, is not to turn you into a traditional shaman, but rather to translate, to help you understand the mysterious and magical world of the shaman, so it will become accessible to the largest possible number of people. The techniques described in this book work just as well in the countryside or in a city, in a desert or in a jungle. We must keep in mind that shamanism is a very down-to-earth art. It is used to solve human problems and to harmonize material and spiritual aspects of your own everyday life.

The philosophies described hereafter also come from great shamanic traditions; we will explain their origins as we go on, when necessary, to help you get a better grasp of the ideas.

Chapter 1

SHAMANISM:
A Spiritual Quest
for Harmony

A Definition of Shamanism

BEFORE anything else, we need to define shamanism and what are shamans. It would be impossible to go any further without this understanding. The historian and philosopher Mircea Eliade considers that shamanism has been practised – and still is – in all areas of the globe, including Europe, Asia, America, Australia, Africa and most of the Pacific Islands.

Shamanism opens up a pathway of knowledge about humans, the universe and the cosmos. It is a different way of perceiving humanity, divinity, nature, as well as a way of connecting them all together. Shamanism is a question of personal power for the individual practising it; it has nothing to do with religious allegiance, but reflects great fundamental principles (which we will examine further on) which connect all shamans together in a brotherhood as ancient as the universe itself.

The fundamental nature of shamanism resides in the practical side of things. First and foremost, it is a natural approach to life, an approach which, all too often, our culture and education makes us lose early on in life. Shamanism is the oldest type of search for knowledge and for the acquisition of personal power which exists on our planet. This type of quest has preceded every religion, every philosophy; it is the foundation of what makes us human beings. Over time, certain techniques and methods were devised to help people learn how to consciously create a bridge between the physical and spiritual realities, between the material world and that of visions.

This apprenticeship does not require any outer intruments, and very little investment of time or money. Does this seem too good to be true? We have a tendancy to believe that simplicity and spirituality do not go hand in hand. This is a quite human defect and, as we will see when we speak about traditional shamanic traditions, many cultures have understood that a long and painstaking learning process is nedded for the student to understand what is really involved. To sum up, one might say that shamanism is a spiritual journey in the lands of our imagination.

The Shaman

Naturally, each population has specific terms to name and describe its own Shamans. In fact, the term "Shaman" belongs to the Tungusic language, whose speakers live in Siberia. It's the term used by all researchers to designate those who practice this art.

We can say that, above all else, a Shaman is a healer; his role is to harmonize the relationship of mind and body, relationships between individuals, between the individual and his environment, between spirit and matter.

In a way he is a link between ordinary humans and gods, or cosmic forces. He is the interface between physical and spiritual realities, being able to change perspective at will; sometimes he even dwells in both.

The reason why the Shaman can thus change perspective, is that he understands that everything that exists is in fact but mere illusion.

It is quite incredible that Shamans had to wait until the end of the XXth century for this basic knowledge, which they possessed for thousands of years, to be validated by science...

Physicists are indeed the ones who, by discovering the atom and its components, finally opened up our eyes. Thus, what seems to us to be matter is not truly so; it is but a mass of microscopic particles gravitating around a central core. From the microcosm up to the macrocosm, everything is similar, it's all a question of perspective.

As you can observe, it's all both simple and complex, as only fundamental truths can be. Essentially, the Shaman trusts his own inner power to draw his own conclusions about a situation; he does not place his trust upon accessories to take a decision.

He may use a variety of tools; herbs, smoke, and so forth to treat a patient, to see in the future, but he does not use these objects to take a decision, to evaluate a situation or to decide upon a course of action.

For a Shaman, it's all a question of perception; his way of seeing things is different from that of most mortals.

The Shaman: a peaceful warrior

This is the most accurate way of describing him. Shamans were always warriors ready to protect and defend the group to which they belonged. But this is not to say that they were always looking to fight. On the contrary they avoided battles and wars. This does not imply that they refused combat however. But they always prefered negotiation over more brutal methods.

To illlustrate this point, we chose a tale from the Japanese tradition, which expreses quite clearly what is a peaceful warrior.

A long time ago there was an inn where thieves awaited visitors in order to kill them during their sleep in order to seize their riches. One day, a warrior came to ask for shelter for the night. This warrior was sure of himself, of his reputation. He believed that nobody would dare hurt him and he fell asleep without taking any precautions. He died in his sleep...

Another warrior, aware of the reputation of this inn, arrived one evening. He told everyone there about the inn's sad reputation; a battle ensued and several innocent people died. The victorious warrior left the battlefield without further ado. The thieves, who had managed to escape, returned and continued to stay in the inn.

A third warrior, passing nearby, knew about the inn's reputation. He cut down a tree to block off the path which led to the place, and continued along his way.

The peaceful warrior does not head straight into trouble, but, when possible, warns in a subtle way those who might be in danger.

The Shaman is also a peaceful warrior; he must comply with rules of ethics, live according to his own code of honour, one that is not rigid but enables him to live in harmony with the universe.

The Shaman's code of honour

● BALANCE :

FINDING THE MIDDLE PATH

Although gravity is the cement which keeps the universe together, balance is what opens up the pathway to its secrets. This rule of balance applies to our body, mind, emotions and to all levels of our being.

This rule reminds us that we always can do too much or too little of anything, which puts into motion the pendulum of our unhealthy habits and of our most destructive models.

If we go too far one way, the pendulum will unavoidably return the other way.

● CHOICE :

TAKING ONE'S POWER INTO OUR OWN HANDS

We are both blessed and cursed by the responsibility implied by our free will. Our future is largely determined by the choices we make here and now.

We cannot always control circumstances; however, we can always choose how we react to them.

By taking this power into our own hands, we discover the courage that we need to live fully.

● PRESENCE :

LIVING IN THE PRESENT

Time is a paradox the reality of which lies in our heads. It stands between a past and a future, one that is too late and the other in the process of becoming.

The concept of time is a convention which helps us ground our thinking.

Nevertheless we can neither see into the past which is not more nor in the future which is yet to be. We are alive only in the present moment.

● COMPASSION :

BECOMING FULLY HUMAN

The universe does not judge; nevertheless, it provides lessons by the way of events. It ofers us the opportunity to balance our karma, to enable us to understand, to assimilate and to actualize what we must learn in order to grow and to become better people.

Compassion enables us to realize that we are doing our best, given our personal capacities and our present beliefs.

● Hope :

EXPANDING ONE'S REALITY

Energy follows the course of our thoughts; we go towards what we imagine, but we cannot go further than what we hope for.

What we expect, hope for or believe creates and colours our experiences. By widening our field of beliefs, our perceptions about what is possible, we are litterally transforming our perspective, and thus our destiny.

● **INTEGRITY :**

LIVING ACCORDING TO ONE'S OWN TRUTH

Integrity implies acting and living in accordance with one's own basic beliefs and the laws of the universe, and this, despite our desire to transgress them once in a while. From this integrity arises our inner reality, the expression of which inspires others not through words, but through example.

● **UNITY :**

EVERYTHING IS CONNECTED

In the same way as raindrops falling from the sky merge into the ocean, we are not separate; rather, we are all a part of the universe, of God. The greatest truth is that we all belong to a great big family; whatever affects anyone among us will have repercussions, to a certain extent, on everyone else.

These are simple rules, but they offer a way of living which can help us to be autonomous and at the same time aware that we are not alone.

Why does one become a Shaman?

There are just as many reasons for this as there are people wishing to become Shamans. There is therefore no such thing as a truly right or wrong answer.

A person becomes a Shaman because she feels the need for it, to put it quite simply. The rest is nothing more than a series of justifications in order to explain this need, which is in fact a vital desire to free oneself from the material constraints which influence and shape our existence, in order to exercise our own personal power over our own life, and over our environment.

This desire might be triggered by any striking event in our life. Often this is a traumatizing experience: an accident, a surgical operation, a long illness, a near-death experience during which one is declared to be clinically dead for a few instants.

In these cases, the desire to become a Shaman becomes obvious, since during one of these important events, the individual becomes aware that the reality in which we are living is artificial, illusory. For these people, a traditional initiation is not necessary: they have pierced the veil of illusion. The rigorous apprenticeship through numerous and often traumatizing initiations is then quite superfluous.

But, historically, a brutal learning process, painful initiations and the absorption of hallucinogenic plants were part of the raidtional training followed by Shamans.

In fact, during several thousand years, end even nowadays, this is the way they are taught. We do not deem it necessary to suffer, to undergo a painful training process or to take drugs in order to pierce the veil of illusions.

Our approach is that of softness, of a knowledge that is slowly acquired when we are ready to assimilate it.

The powers of the inner pathway are within each of us: the way to put them into motion is part of our personal responsibility.

Shamanic Specialties

Historically, Shamans have played various roles: sacred artist, poet, musician, mediator, musician, master of rituals, dancer, singer, etc., depending on the period when they were living as well as the culture they belonged to. For example, the bards of Ancient Gaul were druidic Shamans; the Native American Medicine Man was a Shaman; the African drum-beater was also a Shaman; psychic surgeons in the Philipine Islands are Shamans. Nevertheless there are four shamanic specialties. Here they are.

Healing

Shamans who specialize in this field emphasize the use and study of medicinal herbs and of their properties. They focus on rituals which are directly intended to balance the body and sustain health. They become masters of the energy of healing.

The acquisition of lost
or hidden knowledge

Shamans spend most of their time seeking knowledge that has been lost for centuries. They are also masters at adapting the ancient methods to our modern world and thus to make the survival of shamanic traditions possible. They are the depositories of this knowledge.

The manipulation of power

Shamans are what might be called magicians. They see the currents of energy whch make the realization of coming events possible. They can also influence these currents for the purpose of concretizing projects. The learn to manipulate their personal power and to influence the material world.

Prophecy and clairvoyance

For quite a long time, this was a vital specialty for the tribes. Imagine how important it is to forecast the weather, to know that a agiven region will be fruitful hunting ground, to foresee coming dangers.

As we will see later, all Shamans practice these four specialties; however, one of them may reveal itself to be more pleasant or easier to access. A fact to be noted, all these specialties are connected to the artistic talents of the Shaman since, as you will be able to notice for yourself, several exercises are connected to arts. In fact, we can safely assert that you must develop your artistic talents in order to enjoy your Shamanic gifts.

Shamanic Knowledge, Attributes and Qualities

The knowledge held by Shamans transcends religions, races etc. What enables them to break these barriers is a series of specific skills common to all practitioners of Shamanism, whatever their culture, their religious affiliation, their race, their language, etc. It is the knowledge of these skills which binds together shamanic perception and enables him or her to go beyond the limits of the material world. Along with this knowledge come a series of attributes and qualities which are an integral part of the Shaman. Since it is impossible to split these three facets apart, we have brought them together into one whole, to give an idea of the Shaman's know-how and of the qualities which he acquires by practising his art.

- **The Shaman is familliar with energy and he knows how it works both in the environment and inside the body.**
  He recognizes the power that lies in nature and his connection to it. He knows his spiritual body and can communicate with it to stay healthy and get additional energy when needed.

- **The Shaman has learnt to relax his physical body and to reduce the level of stress it is subjected to so it may be more receptive and effective.**
  He is able to emtpy his mind and silence the voice of his own consciousness in order to better see, hear a, d perceive the messages coming from inside.

23

- **The Shaman uses the power of his inner vision and of his imagination in his trips in search of the knowledge and information that matters to him.**
  He has learnt to recognize the clues and symbols which are given to him along the way to find what he is looking for.
  He believes these clues and symbols to be significant, possessing a meaning which is relevant for his quest.

- **The Shaman has learnt not to judge** or to suspend his judgment in order to listen more closely to his own intuition.

- **The Shaman learns to use images of nature and symbols coming from both the inside and from the outside.**
  He knows how to interpret them in order to solve his problems and to succeed in overcoming the obstacles located along his way.
  Since the Shaman is also an artist, he expresses his symbolism in the form of dances, chants, ritual movements and rythms.

- **The Shaman learns how to understand people and to help them heal.**
  He develops a knowledge of the personality structures of individuals.

- **The Shaman also knows how to laugh.**
  He has learnt to detach himself sufficiently from the trials and tribulations of life to be able to find the humour lying behind the human condition.

- **The Shaman learns to communicate both outwardly and inwardly simultaneously.**
  He masters his situation with one foot in both realities (material and spiritual) without losing sight of what is happening in one or the other.
  This way of living alters his perception of time and also enables him not to believe in the limits of man's spirit.

- **The Shaman learns how to achieve success and he knows exactly when to take action.**
  He does not practice living room philosophy; his philosophy is practical and his training enables him to solve dilemnas. He also feels at ease with paradoxes.

- **The Shaman knnows how to go from one level of consciousness to another, and this, at will.**
  He is just as much at ease meditating as he is wtrolling in the street, these two states of consciousness being examples of all possible states.
  Since he feels at ease at all levels, he is flexible and able to shift from one state of consciousness to another quickly and safely.

- **The Shaman is a Warrior.**
  He is disciplined and perseverant in his quest for personal power, which also makes him quite effective when he uses that power to serve others.

- **The Shaman knows how to protect himself.**
  He can face major obstacles and overcome negative influences without losing sight of his ultimate goal.

This knowledge, and these attributes and qualities are shared by all Shamans, whatever their culture, and throughout the history of humanity.

These quite common individuals developed these qualities through a specific training and discipline.

They were curious and interested by shamanic knowledge and their level of skills, all things considered, was neither higher nor lower than yours.

The Benefits of Shamanism

Because we want to remain faithful to the practical turn of mind which is at the root of Shamanism, we have decided to list the benefits which you will profit from through the practise of this art.

- The perception you have of your own past, and of its influence on your present-day life and that of others, starts to change. Your conscience of linear time as you usually perceive it also changes, which gives you more freedom.

- Your perception of who is responsible for your life is transformed; therefore, you do not feel anymore like you are the victim of events or circumstances.

- Your vision of yourself as an individual separate from your environment is brought into question and you begin to recognize the fact that you are connected to everything that is alive. As a result, your horizons expand.

- Your perception of reality and of its nature, and of how to achieve your goals are all going to be radically transformed. You are going to discover how you can set for yourself goals that are better suited for your nature, and how to achieve them more easily.

- Your understanding of power and of how you can enjoy it is going to be positively transformed and phenomenally increased.

- Your knowledge and your understanding of interpersonal relations is radically altered; moreover, your faculties of communication with others is improved. You perceive differently the idea of compassion, as you understand yourself and others around you more clearly.

- You are going to feel inspired and ready to deal with the challenges and obstacles which you will fell empowered to clear; at the same time, you will be able to avoid those obstacles which are impossible for you to overcome.

- You learn how to gain access to the knowledge and information which you had previously considered inaccessible.

- You learn how to draw energy from a universal and inexhaustible source: the universe. This source will always be available for anyone who knows how to take advantage of it.

- You learn how to relax and not to feel as much stress when facing an obstacle.

The Various Phases of Shamanic Training

To help you understand the process a bit more clearly, here is an insight into what happens when you decide to follow a shamanic training.

In order to develop your skills as a Shaman, you must learn and understand how energy works. Why? The reason is quite simple. The intensity of your thoughts and emotions has a direct influence upon energy, which has effects both in the spiritual and material dimensions. Later on, you can start to become familiar with your spiritual body: what it does for you, how it works and how you can use it. That is when you will start to get a handle on the energies contained in your spiritual body, in such a way that you will constantly be feeling vigorous and powerful.

The following phase consists in grounding yourself, in other words reinforcing your bond with the energies of the Earth. this will enable you to protect yourself from negative or non-beneficial energies, especially when you will be carryiong out shamanic exercises.

Another aspect of shamanic training is to teach you how to gain access to the world of spirit, through tunnels. This training also leads you into building your own pathways to the spirit world, which also helps you gain greater mastery over your personal power.

Studying shamanic practises, is to acquire a system of knowledge which precedes all of the organized lines of organized knowledge of our time. This is a shortcut which litterally cuts through centuries of dogmas and theological theories, through a method which helps you return simply perceiving the universe and the flow of energy through various streams.

One of the assets of our modern world is that of science. Something which would have perceived as pure magic a few centuries ago can sometimes find an explanation through the laws of quantum physics. It is like combining the innocent vision of a child, with the intellect of an adult, nourished by centuries of scientific investigation. In other words, the best of both worlds !

When you practise Shamanism, you become a co-creative part of nature, a catalyst agent for the changes occurring around you. You also realize that this sense of loneliness which dwells insied each of us is but mere illusion, as you discover the links uniting you with all living things. You then experience unparalleled harmony as you integrate yourself into the universe. In doing this, you gradually understand that you are aliging yourself with nature's healing forces. You know who you are and you finally know where you are going.

Chapter 2

The Seven Founding
Principles of Shamanism

HAMANISM is based on seven fundamental principles, and their corollaries which explain and illustrate them. Why seven principles? Because of the nature of that very figure which, in many cultures, is considered as an esoteric, magical number, symbolizing life and the union of the feminine and masculine principles. For ancient civilizations, the 3 symbolizes the primal male force, and the 4 symbolizes the creative female force; these two numbers represent the polarities of the universe. Seven is also related to the seven colors of the rainbow and to several other symbols of the same kind. In Hawaiian, the number 7 is pronounced hiku, hi meaning "flowing from the source", a symbol of the female principle, whereas ku means "holding firm", a symbol of the male principle. The analogies are numerous to illustrate the significance of the number 7 and its connotations of balance between the male principle, yang and female principle, yin, of life itself.

These principles contain a philosophy offering the Shaman the capability of understanding how the universe works, and therefore the ability to manipulate cosmic energies in order to achieve his goals - a material gain or healing of a person's condition for example.

When you start thinking along the lines expressed in this chapter, you are engaged along the shamanic path.

All the exercises we describe have but a single purpose, that of helping you to assimilate the shamnic way of thinking.

We will see further on that, traditionally, it is through the use of drugs and privations that the postulants live out their initiation. The only purpose of this exercise is to radically alter their perception of the world.

As we said earlier, we prefer a more rational approch which enables you to understand the changes that occur and to make choices.

Here are the seven shamanic principles and the corollaries which go along with it.

PRINCIPLE 1 :
The World is
what you Believe it is

It's all a question of perception. The best example of that is the division between those who see a glass as being half empty or half full. The person who sees the glass as half full perceives abundance, whereas the one who sees it as half empty anticipates lack. That might seem overly simplistic to you; but the greatest principles are often the simplest. It is their very simplicity which prevents us from realizing how significant they are. For a Shaman, everything is a question of perspective: a different point of view creates different expectations and desires, and these emotions have repercussions upon the world of the spirits.

For example, rainfalls are most often beneficial for crops and the growth of plants. If you have a garden, you will perceive summer showers as something positive. However, if you plan to have a picnic out in the counrtyside, the very same showers will seem to you to be an nuisance: they're quite likely to ruin your pleasure.

The shamanic vision, is firstly to see the two sides of the coin and to understand that a given thing, event or circumstance will become positive or negative depending on who is considering it. Everything depends on how you think. If we go too far along this direction, we can also see that thoughts of fear, anxiety and holding a grudge can litterally make someone ill

by undermining their energy and diminshing their efficiency. Everything depends upon your expectations. If
they are negative, you run the risk of living with even
more anxiety, fear and resentment. However, thoughts
of self-confidence, trust, love, determinationand the
ability to forgive can help you recover your health,
balance and stability. If your expectations are positive,
this message will reverberate into the etheric world
and the energies which will return towards you will be
positive.

COROLLARY 1 :

All is but a dream

If everything depends on your perspective, where is
reality? If the latter changes depending on how you
think, almost depending on your mood, where does it
hide? This amounts to asking the existential question :
"Am I a human being dreaming he is a butterfly or a
butterfly dreaming he is a human being?" When you
travel in the world of dreams, the univers you're in is
just as real as the one you move around in during your
waking hours, or is it the other way around? For thousands of years, we believed matter to be solid. XXth
century physics, with the discovery of the atom, helped us clearly understand that matter was a mere illusion; we have the illusion that a table is solid, but in
fact it is made up of atoms which are themselves made
up of even more tiny particles gravitating around a
central nucleus. The apparent solidity of matter is but
a mere illusion.

For the Shaman, memory is made up of dreams. For him, daily reality is but a mass illusion. Let's say that this so-called "reality" is a dream shared by a great number of people. Therefore, since life is but a dream, and since the memories we have are also dreams, it is possible to change them. When you dream, it sometime happens that you realize the fact that you are dreaming, and at that stage it is possible for you to control what is going on. When you become a Shaman, you learn to change the quality of your dreams and you influence the quality of your ordinary existence, by transforming them.

COROLLARY 2 :
All systems are arbitrary

There again, it's all a question of perspective. You can start out from the principle that life is beautiful. Such an assertion can generate some disagreement if one of your partners considers that life is valley of tears. Where is the truth?

Life can be both; for some, it's a valley of tears and for others, it's paradise. But that's not all there is to it. A person who considers that life is but a valley of tears can seem to possess everything they could need to be happy. A person's happiness can be another's misery. Organized religions insist that they are in possession of the truth; and yet, one's truth can be another's heresy. Truth is more of a complex mosaic, constantly fluctuating.

For the Shaman, reality is what he decides it to be, since everything is a dream. Therefore, absolute truth is what he decides it to be. Truth is arbitrary, since it depends on what you are presently thinking; it also depends on your experience, and on how you interpret it. It is also your choice to accept the interpretation and vision of another individual or group of individuals. Therefore, the existence of every system depends on the acceptance by a group of people of a certain interpretation of the truth, which they all agree upon. For the Shaman, it's all very simple. If a truth suits you, use it; if it does not suit you, if a given interpretation prevents you from moving forward, simply find another one. This corollary makes the Shaman very tolerant towards other systems, since they are all arbitrary and can all be of service towards good. The Shaman is not in possession of the absolute truth and its principles.

PRINCIPLE 2:
There are no Limits

At first sight, this idea might seem bizarre, even absurd, because we are constantly experiencing limitations; we can only grow to a certain height, the planet has a limited size, our eyes see in a certain way, we only possess a given amount of money in the bank, and so on.

And yet, if we accept the first principle – the world is what we believe it to be – the universe is limitless. It could not be any other way in order to satisfy all experiences, all of the thoughts of every creature. So, you might argue, if the universe is illimited, why must we constantly be experiencing our own limits? It must be specified that there exist two types of limits: creative limits and filtered limits.

Creative limits enable us to experience a certain reality. For example, to experience the material world, the physical universe, we have to set certain standards in order to create a reality which is sufficiently wide to contain all of humanity. Therefore, in order to live in our physical reality, we have to take into account the fact that our senses possess a range of perceptions which is limited to certain sound frequencies, or light frequencies; we also have to take into account our limited possibilities in terms of touch, attraction and gravity, perception of time and distance, just to mention the main ones. Humanity has also invented machines which help it go further away, and some people have extra-sensory thanks to which they can transcend the limits we just mentionned. However, these creative limits are essential to experience material reality.

It is therefore fair and reasonnable to say that certain limits are necessary, simply to exist in our terrestrial universe. One maight also add that these creative limitsgive us the opportunity to improve ; our personal creative skills by enabling us to focus our energies on a certain range of experiences. The best analogy taht comes to mind is that of a chess-player and his sixty-four squares ; it might seem simple on the outset, but we must never lose sight of the fact that the human mind has not yet been able to find all of the possible combinations in the game of chess. So, what might appear at first to be limited is perhaps not as much so as we might have thought.

Filtered limits, on the other hand, are imposed upon us by ideas and beliefs that restrain our creativity. The best examples of this type of limits are the beliefs or dogmas which make you feel powerless or desperate, or those that turn around vengeance or cruelty. For example, consider someone who would be constantly raging and yelling against the universe, because it allows injustice and misery to exist. Such a person is powerless with regard to all of this distress, and she perpetuates it, through her obsession with injustice. She feels desperate and powerless in front of life's implacable circumstances. Any belief which makes you powerless is harmful. Filtered limits are those that focus your energies on problems, while at the same time considering that you are unable to change or do anything about them. The Shaman remains far removed from the beliefs and limits that disempower him.

COROLLARY 1 :
Everything is connected

In several Shamanic traditions, this idea is illustrated by a spider's web. The Shaman becomes in a way the spider weaving the web of his existence. The latter is not only that of his own life, but it is also connected to all other webs which represent life around him, in a continuum that includes all living things on our planet. Because of this link, a mere positive or negative thought influences, to a certain extent, all other webs. It is this link that enables the Shaman to heal or influence those around him.

COROLLARY 2 :
Everything is possible

If there are no limits, one can then say that every-thing is possible, that all you need to do is to believe. Nevertheless, since you are not alone in the universe, what you can share with those around you depends upon their beliefs. For example, you may use your hea-ling powers on certain people, whereas on others, this is completely impossible because they do not believe one bit in all of this. Remember that even the Christ had trouble doing miracles in his native village: the people around him had trouble believing that this would be possible for the son of a carpenter.

COROLLARY 3:
Related but independant

This is a major illusion, as some people can become overwhelmed by the idea that everything is connected. If you are afraid that the least of your thoughts is bound to influence the people around you, you won't be able to do anything anymore. Your fear of taking action will make you forget that you are a dream-weaver. What you have to understand is that although everything is connected, you still have free-will. You are independant, and your role as a dream-weaver can help people around you; you must learn to be compassionate. The rule that there are no real limits can also help you create certain limits that will help you in your daily actions.

PRINCIPLE 3:
Energy Flows
Wherever you Focus
your Awareness

To illustrate this principle, we must mention the privileged use by Shamans of meditation and hypnosis, which work in accordance to the previously mentioned principle.

Meditation is used in many cultures and religions, and means something different for each of them.

For some, meditation brings to mind the image of a monk, alone in his cell, in communion with God.

Others will envision a Zen temple, where the ranks of novices are motionless, under the vigilant scrutiny of a guard.

Others still will think of a group of yuppies sitting in circles, chanting mantras in some unknown language.

Whatever idea or image comes to mind for you, realize that what is at hand here is a different sort of meditation for each of the individuals or groups concerned.

Meditation is quite simply the action of thinking deeply and continuously, in other words focusing your awareness for a certain amount of time.

Therefore, you are meditating whenever you focus your awareness onto an object for a long time.

According to the philosophy of the Shamans, this awareness, this concentration, channels the energy of the universe, making it possible to materialize whatever you are focusing on. This meditation also includes your expectations and desires, and you must learn how to reconcile all the various parts of your awareness in order to fully allow the object of your meditation to be materialized.

Hypnosis is also a technique which helps you focus your awareness for a certain amount of time. It is similar to meditation, but many people consider them to be different techniques.

Most people consider meditation to be more spiritual than hypnosis; they use meditation to get free from their karma, to find God; they would use hypnosis to stop smoking or to lose weight.

For the Shaman, establishing such distinctions is illusory; he uses both of these techniques.

Remember: the Shaman uses whatever works best.

The only difference is that for hypnosis, you need a person, or a cassette, to help you focus your awareness; meditation is more personal. It must be specified though that self-hypnosis tends to abolish that difference.

What matters, is to remember that energy flows wherever you focus your awareness.

If your life is satisfying, everthing is fine; if, however, your life is not what you would like it to be, you must change the points on which you are focusing. Hypnosis and meditation are excellent tools to do that.

COROLLARY 1 :

Everything is energy

This is not a major discovery for most of us. Modern physics has helped us understand this for several decades now.

However, if everything is energy, thoughts are also energy; since one kind of energy can be converted into another kind – think of hydro-electric power plants, which convert magnetic energy into electricity -, the energy of our thoughts can be, in the same way, converted into their material equivalent.

PRINCIPLE 4:
Now is the Moment
of Power

According to several Eastern traditions, your present existence is a result of your actions and decisions made during past lifetimes.

For example, if your past lives were good, you will have a good life; if, on the contrary, you were a tyrant, you will experience pain and hardships in your present lifetime.

Such is the law of karma, the law of retribution, the law of action and reaction.

These days, there are several Western traditions which are re-writing these ancient traditions.

One of them asserts that you experience the retribution of karma in your present lifetime; for all your actions, you experience a counter-action; if you transgress a law, you will almost instantly be punished.

Another tradition believes that your behavior depends upon your heredity, your education, and your childhood. It implies that you are the product of uncontrollable forces for which you cannot be held responsible.

There are several ways to consider your present existence. Here is how Shamans see it.

For a Shaman, it is not the past which causes what you are now, or what you possess. Rather, it is the beliefs, decisions and actions you are having or taking this very moment, right now, with respect to your environment, which turn you into what you are, or which cause you to be the owner of your present-day possessions.

Karma exists, and it is in the present moment that it is active.

Your environment and your surroundings are the reflection of your mental and physical behavior right now, at this present instant.

We owe it to our memory to have the possibility of continuously adopting the same habits from one day to the next, but each day is a new creation and any habit can be changed in the present. This might not be necessarily easy, but it is possible indeed.

Your genes are not what determines what you are, but a part of you which determines which characteristics best reflect your beliefs and intentions.

COROLLARY 1 :
Everything is relative

It's quite nice to be able to say : "now is the moment of power", but how are we to define what is "now" ?

The simplest and most practical way to do so is to determine the scope of your present awareness. This means that "now" can be a second, a minute, an hour, a day, a month, depending on what is your goal or purpose. This also implies, once in a while, that "now" can contain a part of the past and of the future. This is fine, since we must not lose sight of the fact that this future is relative to the moment when we are having that thought; the same is true for the past. Take the time to write about it, and the past and future have already changed and shifted.

As you can see, everyhting depends upon the scope of your awareness, and on your focusing power. Everything is relative.

COROLLARY 2:

Power increases as you focus on your senses

No need to be a Shaman to know that everywhere around us, there are people who are not fully there.

Their awareness is caught in the past or in the future; they are never present, their heads hover in the clouds.

This kind of behavior diminishes their awareness of the present moment and reduces their power for action.

You can lose yourself regularly, or once in a while, to change your outlook; when you escape from the present moment to plan, to look for inspiration, to relax, this type of change is even beneficial.

However, it can be damageable to do this all the time; you might reach a point of no return, or lose your effectiveness once you come back down to Earth. Some people are completely obsessed by, or lost in their past, or in parallel universes, because of some fear, or anger. Guilt, resentment or anxiety are often the agents which cause them to escape from the present, away from the simple joys of life. Most of these fears and anger can be cleared by deciding to examine the present moment.

What we mean, is to become more fully aware of what your senses are feeling, here and now.

Remember the third principle: energy flows wherever you focus your awareness.

As you focus your awareness on your senses and on the information conveyed by them, you can experience moments of extreme sensory acuity and become aware of all of the energy flowing around you.

You become aware that many things are happening in your immediate surroundings, which is a bit like awakening from a long sleep, and becoming aware that you are in a dream, and that you have the power to change it.

PRINCIPLE 5:
Loving Implies
Being Satisfied in Love

This concept has become trite and a commonplace cliché! We love peanut butter, our parents, our new car. We express an extremely wide range of ideas and intentions through these simple words: sexual desire, pleasure, possession, possessiveness, need, neediness, dependency, etc. As we listen to popular songs or as we read novels, we see love often being defined as a kind of illness. Love must be defined from a Shamanic point of view, as a quite simple concept in itself.

Love can only exist if we are happy with the object of our love. In any relationship, whatever the object of our desire – a person, a place, an object – happiness comes from the love we feel. Misery comes from the fear, anger and doubts which we might be feeling around that relationship. Hence, it is not because we love someone that we have "sticky hands", but rather because we are afraid of something, afraid, for example, of being rejected or of seeming ridiculous. Similarly, loving in itself is not harmful in any way: what causes pain is the anger we feel when our love is not returned. What we get from being in love is joy; the intensity of that joy will depend upon the depth of our feelings. Being deeply in love implies being profoundly connected to each other; the depth and purity of that feeling and of the bond will increase as fear, doubt and anger subside.

COROLLARY 1 :
Love increases
when we stop judging

Love is always there, always present; unfortunately, there is often a layer of fear, anger and doubt covering it up.

These three elements - fear, anger and doubt - give rise to negative criticism and to unfounded judgement, which cause separation and diminish our capacity to love.

Criticism is often responsible for the death of relationships.

Conversely, compliments can build and reconstruct the latter, because they are motions of love which express that we are feeling well with someone. This assertion reinforces the relationship.

This principle is so simple : when you make compliments, you are reinforcing the positive aspect of the relationship : it grows and expands.

When you criticize, you are reinforcing the negative aspect, those things you do not like : unfortunately, that aspect is the one which which then begins to grow and expand.

A new relationship is generally filled with joy, pleasure and excitement, as you have the tendency not to notice the small defects or to consider them as negligible. As doubts settle in about you, about your partner or even about the relationship, this is the time when criticisms start to surface and imagination can play a negative role. When this happens early on, the relationship is short-lived. When these elements emerge gradually, we see a relationship which deteriorates until one of the partners cannot stand it anymore.

In both cases, the relationship contained more pain than pleasure. When a relationship is ailing because of criticism, it can be saved by stopping it and replacing it by compliments. Both partners must be aware and in agreement.

COROLLARY 2 :
Everything is alive, conscious and sentient

For a Shaman, life is not limited to plants, animals and humans; it includes everything which moves, even if these movements remain imperceptible to our senses.

For a Shaman, this is just a matter of different forms of life.

Since the source of life is infinite and since this source is aware of itself, everything which exists is conscious to a certain extent, and therefore, is sensitive, at one level or another, to what is going on around it.

This is why the Shaman respects everything which exists.

Your subconscious is alive, conscious and sensitive.

When you criticize yourself, he perceives these attacks and tries to defend itself, often by tensing up your muscles, which induces stress and interferes with your consciousness, your memory and energy flow. This reaction is often the cause of illness and accidents. A small criticism will not cause all of this damage; it's more the habit of constantly critizing yourself which creates problems. The opposite is also true. The habit of praising yourself relaxes your muscles, increases your awareness, your energy flow and your strength, improves your memory and, generally speaking, enables you to feel better.

The mechanism is quite simple. When you criticize, whether it be yourself, your car, the government, etc., several things happen.

Firstly, you must understand that your subconscious does not make the difference between you and others. Whether you are criticizing the rain, yourself or another person, your subconscious takes it personnally and your body tenses up. On the other hand, when you praise whomever or whatever, your body relaxes because your subconscious also takes it personnally.

Secondly, according to the third principle, whatever the characteristic on which your bring your awareness to bear, it attracts energy. Therefore, if you criticize, what you are criticizing will be strengthened; the oppopsite is also true; a compliment reinforces the positive aspect.

Thirdly, your critical attitude makes you withdraw

from the present, forces you to flee, which decrreases your efficiency and your capacity to transform your reality.

What can you do if you are the target of constant criticism ?

If someone is criticizing your looks, your clothes or whatever, reply by making a compliment on the same topic.

This will have the effect of neutralizing negative forces.

PRINCIPLE 6:
All Power Comes from Within

Most existing religions or philosophies teach that we are relatively insignificant, that true power belongs to the gods or at least that it lies outside of our own control, because it is in the possession of governments, or authorities, that we are reliant upon our genes, our culture, etc. Shamanism on the contrary teaches us that the real power which creates our experience originates in our body, our spirit and our conscious mind.

Logically, if the universe is limitless, if the source of life is infinite, its power is therefore ever present, everywhere, including the place where we are right now.

Practically, nothing could happen to us without our taking part in it, one way or another.

You attract the events which occur in your life through your beliefs and desires, fears and expectations. Then, you react either in accordance with your habits, or in a conscious manner.

Noone is actually making you miserable. You make yourself miserable because the people around you are not reacting in the way you would like them to.

If you have been hurt or mistreated, it is crucial for you to realize that there is a part of you which attracted towards you this type of behavior.

Which is not to say that you are to be blamed for these events. In most cases, you were not aware of the beliefs and attitudes which got you in that situation in the first place.

Nor is this to be an excuse for the person who mis-treated you, supposedly because his beliefs led him to behave as he did.

You are not a mere victim of events, and you can take an active part in them, and transform them.

COROLLARY 1 :
Everything is powerful

Sometimes when we begin to experience the concept of power and the fact that we can create our own experience, we believe we are the only individual involved and that noone else could intervene in our universe.

This would amount to shifting from one extreme to another : starting out from the concept that we have no power and tilting to the other extreme, whereby we would possess all of the power existing in the world. Everyone possesses the same capacity; whatever the event, each and every participant in thaht event is creating their own experience. Everyone has the same power.

We'll even go further. Everything has the same power : the trees, the wind, the flowers, the stars, etc., everything in existence has this power. If you think about this a little bit, you will see that the opposite is impossible to prove as being true.

From this point of view, you can understand why it is better to work in conjunction with the forces of nature, with everything in existence, rather than imposing your own will upon objects which you consider to be inanimate.

For a Shaman, everything is powerful and he must learn to use the power of his allies.

Traditionally, the Shaman learns how to use the power of trees, of the wind; nowadays, in an urban context, he will learn for example to use the power of computers, of technology, of music.

Power is everywhere, and each and every form or source of power can be useful.

COROLLARY 2:
Power comes from authority

To simplify this concept, let's say that there are two types of authority: outer authority and inner authority.

When you place your decision-making faculty into the hands of another person, you have an outer authority; however, if you keep your own decision-making faculty, you have inner authority, which is much more sound.

This concept is reinforced by considering that one of the basic forms of power is authority. When someone speaks with authority, they speak with conviction and self-confidence.

When God created the light, He said: "Let there be light!" This was an affirmation, not a "maybe". This is the very secret of any prayer, incantation or invocation.

Words are powerful, to the extent that they are uttered with authority.

No half-measure, no maybes or whining; to be effective, these affirmations must be uttered with trust, authority and faith.

When you pray, lay aside any sense of persecution or any complaints, and be assertive as you speak.

PRINCIPLE 7 :
Efficiency is the Measure of Truth

To the contrary of what you might believe, the end does not justify the means. The means are what determines the end.

Brutal, violent means will produce violent results ; peaceful means will bring about peaceful results.

Achieving success through pitiless or cruel means will cause you to live in an environment where others behave in a similar way with regards to you.

If, on the contrary, you achieve success by helping others, this will produce an atmosphere where your success will be acclaimed and supported by others.

This principle also explains why the true Shaman will use the methods which work for him or for the individual coming to seek his help.

The Shaman, is not searching for the absolute truth ; these are realities which have no significance for him.

The Shaman is essentially practical-minded ; he will not hesitate to use the herbs, plants, tools and rituals which suit him, whatever their origin may be.

All concepts, - Christinanity, Buddhism, Wicca - may serve a purpose depending on the opportunity. The Shaman's goal is to heal, to serve, and for that he's on the lookout for efficiency, which becomes his main criterion.

COROLLARY 1 :
There is always another way
of doing things

Every problem has more than one solution. In a universe without limits, things could not be any different.

Unfortunately, people often stay blocked with one method, one technique, one way of doing things, one plan to achieve success. And if this method does not work for them, they simply give up and quit.

If your goal is significant, you should not give up. If a given method does not work, you might simply need to change your technique or approach.

For example, if your were using a physical approach, simply try another approach, a more spiritual or emotional one for instance.

There are so many examples of this. The ways you can improve your own life and life in general are infinitely varied; there are always new ones which you did not yet have a chance to try out, and which you probably have not yet even heard of.

Chapter 3

Your First Steps
along the Shamanic Path

E have devised two major steps in the shamanic training, with several exercises in each. You can follow them in the order we established, or in any other way that suits you better, as you wish. These steps and exercises will lead you to change your perception of the world, of reality. If you feel more comfortable to begin by the exercises in the second step, feel free to do so. What matters, is to achieve a new perspective, that of a Shaman in tune with the seven principles listed earlier on. This new way of thinking and looking at reality will enable you to live in harmony with nature and with everything that lives and breathes.

FIRST STEP:
Meeting
your Animal Guide

The Native American Method

Now that we know the basic principles of the shamanic philosophy, we are going to begin the exercises in the shamanic pathway.

The Shaman possesses an ally, a guide who helps him to communicate more easily with the spiritual world.

We chose the Native American method because it is easy and well known by many people; the idea is to meet one's totem animal.

Native Americans are not the only ones to choose an ally in the animal world; several other traditions in Africa, and others still in Scandinavia, have this same sort of guide. Since the Native American method is the most documented one, it is the one we advise you to adopt. It is safe and risk-free.

As you will observe, this is a process which requires time and perseverance.

This quite extraordinary experience connects you to an animal who becomes a npart of you.

This totem is in fact a spiritual guide who will help you in an unimaginable way.

Different methods

There are different methods to get in touch with your totem animal. In ancient times, young warriors went out into the woods for several days of fasting and meditation. After a sleepless night, on the morning of the third day, the first animal whom the youth saw that day was considered to be his totem. If we practise this kind of ritual in a city, our totem might run the risk of being a pigeon, or the neighbor's cat.

Certain tribes used and are still using the "ritual sauna" (or sweatlodge) to obtain this sort of vision. After several hours, the young seeker has a vision in which his totem animal's identity is revealed to him. He is then able to hold conversations with it.

Other tribes resorted to hallucinogenic drugs for the person to take on his totem's characteristics. This type of experience is not to be reommended; the problems that can result from it are much greater than the possible benefits. One must keep in mind that if your vision is distorted because of the use of drugs or alcohol, your totem animal will be unable to reply.

We offer you herebelow a relatively simple method which will help you get acquainted with your totem. Everyone can have a totem animal. Animals and spirits do not recognize the differences we make between peoples and races. If you truly wish the help of a totem animal, it will be granted to you, quite simply.

Purification of the body

A body purification ritual is essential before starting.

- Use a natural cedar or pine soap, and remain under the shower for at least two minutes, enough time to allow the water to cover you completely.

  This action has the effect of completely purifying your aura from any foreign particles.

- If you take a bath, add a few drops of pine extract essential oil.

  Make sure you immerse yourself entirely for a few seconds.

  Once this is done, dry yourself.

- Now, burn some sage leaves and wrap yourself up in the smoke.

  Use a mixture of sage and pine as incense.

  You may listen to some traiditional Indian music.

- If you feel the need to wear clothes, dress up comfortably with natural fibers: cotton, linen, silk.

- It is preferable to be lying down for this exercise in order to maximise your degree of relaxation.

  Make sure you will not be disturbed for a period of approximately one hour.

The encounter persay

Settle in comfortably, practise a relaxation exercise, as thoroughly as possible.

- Relax each part of your own body, going slowly, from head to toes.
  Any time you sense any troublesome thoughts, take a deep inbreath, slowly breathing out, while focusing on the oxygen being absorbed.

- Imagine that you are in a forest; take the time to visualize clearly where you are, stroll around, relax.

- You arrive in front of a huge tree; this could very well be a gnarled oak tree or a Western red pine tree, an enormous tree.

Being able to receive cosmic energies as trees do.

- In fact, this tree is so huge that it has an opening between its roots. You immediately feel attracted by this. It is large enough so you may introduce yourself in it free from any risk or fear.

- You enter into the tree's core and there you find a well. You are curious and therefore come nearer and let yourself fall into this well. The descent has nothing frightening about it; it's rather a pleasant experience, something like a gigantic slipping down. You have the impression of gliding, without any fear or expectations. You are very satisfied with your situation, you are having a marvelous experience.

- You reach the end of the tunnel. You come out of it and notice that once again you are in a forest. Sit at the foot of a tree and wait; in a while, your totem animal will come and speak to you. You are now in a universe where you are able to communicate with him.

- You remain there, or you go for a walk, it does not matter: your totem will know where to find you. Let your guide come to you. Once he is by your side, you will easily discover how to communiocate with him. He will be able to answer all of your questions and to help you follow your Shamanic path.

CHARACTERISTICS OF THE TOTEM ANIMALS

Here is a list of the most common totems. We have drawn it from the Native American traditions, but your animal totem may come from another part of the globe.

The totem animal is a guide, chosen in order ot help you. His qualities match your needs in terms of Shamanic initiation.

An elephant's memory might be what you need, or else the qualities of a tiger...

You can even have as a totem a mythical animal, a unicorn or a griffin.

Once again, one must not forget that everything is possible; therefore, do not limit yourself by choosing in advance an animal without knowing if he suits you or not. Let the universe choose for you.

EAGLE

He represents the powers of spirit. He can travel throughout the spiritual realm while remaining in touch with Earth and matter. His faculties of observation and his courage are legendary. This is demanding guide who will ask you to supervise him constantly, to go further and always higher.

SPIDER

He is the weaver of the dreams of humankind. His web encompasses everything that lives; he weaves the fate of men and of all creatures. He is a guide who enables you to mastere the art of weaving dreams and reality in a blend which will reveal itself to be positive for your realizations. With his help, you will learn to materialize your desires and to dream your life.

DEER

He is gentle; his nature reveals an inexhaustible treasure of compassion and love which enable him to ignore fear. The deer perceives the kindness which lies in every creature, in even the most desperate situations. This guide teaches the power of gentleness; he shows his apprentice how to touch the heart and minds of even the most hardened of all creatures and how to help them heal.

BAT

His qualities are mythical. They represent reincarnation, the cycle of death and rebirth. This is a guide who will help you to accept the end of any situation and the new possibilities that are emerging. He is also a reliable ally to travel into the universe of one's past lives.

DOG

This guide is the emblem of loyalty. He cannot help but come to the rescue of others. If the dog becomes your guide, you will be called to serve others, whatever your line of work. He teaches you the purest kind of friendship, with him you will learn unconditional love.

CROW

This is a sacred animal for several cultures. It is the guardian of magic, of esoteric knowledge, of timeless wisdom.

He teaches you to overcome your fears of the unknown, as well as many deep-seated fears hiding at the back of one's consciousness. He is the guide who transports you directly into the world of the spirits to enable you to reach quickly higher levels of awareness.

COYOTE

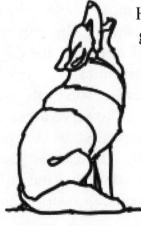

He is the most unpredictable of all guides. His nature is to play tricks; he often gets lost in complex strategies and falls into his own snares.

He teaches you to laugh at your own misfortunes and to choose the good side of life, whatever the circumstances may be. He teaches you how to see through your own lies, and recognize your onw conditionings.

HAWK

He is the Messenger of the Gods, a scout who oversees his domain through the airs to check what is going on. He pays particular attention to details and can grasp all nuances in any situation. This guide will help you develop your extra-sensory perceptions. With him, you will learn that your power depends on the acuteness of your perceptions.

OWL

He is associated to psychic faculties: clairvoyance, astral projection, etc. He symbolizes magical practices. With the owl as a guardian, you will be attracted by the practice of magic. He will also help you achieve wisdom if you remain on the Shamanic path. He will also help you be aware when others are trying to deceive you.

DRAGONFLY

This the messenger of dreams, the one who shows you how to recognize the illusion of what we name "reality". The wings of a dragonfly enable you to recognize various levels of dreams and bring up to the surface buried memories. This guide enables you to communicate with creatures related to the elements.

UNICORN

Although of European origin, the unicorn is a powerful guide who becomes the ally of individuals whose goals and ideals are pure and difficult to attain. This is a guide who enables you to reach incredible peaks at the service of others.

HARE

He represents fear and tragedy but, deep inside of himself, he possesses the capacity to overcome them. This is a guide who will make you travel into every nook and crany of your worst fears in order to confront them. He also enables you to detect danges surrounding you and to recognize individuals whith evil intentions.

LION

He empowers you to lead a group in a positive way and without any excessive thirst for power. His courage is aften an asset in difficult times.

WOLF

He is the sentry, one who goes ahead of the others to choose the best route. He is also the one who innovates, who discovers new secrets and shares them. Like the dog, he is very loyal to his group; however, he is a natural-born loner. You will learn to cultivate detachment while preserving close ties with your surroundings.

OTTER

She is often the yin totem par excellence. Her energy is feminine, but it can act as a guide both for men and women. This is a very motherly guide, who takes good care of her apprentices. Her curiosity is legendary and she shares it quite willingly. She teaches us how to get rid of our preconceptions, prejudice, and doubts about others.

LYNX

He holds secrets and it is difficult to make him speak. He has the power to travel through time and space; he can open all doors to the past. The hardest task is to tame him, to make him understand that you are worthy of sharing his secrets, his teachings. He teaches you to see what others are hiding, their fears and doubts.

BEAR

He is the king of introspection; he is constantly searching for the truth, eager for the secrets of Earth and nature. His way of learning is to sleep deep down in a cave during winter, where he is directly in touch with the Earth's energies. He is the master of dreams and of the solutions conveyed by them.

BUTTERFLY

He is an agent of transformation. He teaches the person he is guiding how to change his perceptions of the world and of those around him. The butterfly is an unparalleled guide for Shamans dedicating themselves to the healing arts. He also helps us understand the many changes which occur during our lives.

SNAKE

This is a terribly unrecognized creature who has an important place in the world of Shamans. Those who have suach a guide are very rare indeed, and the knowledge of a snake is mysterious: it has to do with immortality, and psychic energy. His knowledge is ancient, more ancient than History, and he is gifted with knowledge.

TURTLE

This is the most ancient Native American symbol for the Earth. This guide has a shell which protects him and he teaches you how to protec yourself from blows, envy jealousy and the unconsciousness of those around you. This does not mean you have to retire from the world; on the contrary, this protection enables you to help others more easily.

As you can observe, the characteristics listed hereabove are but a short summary of the powers and capacities of totem animals.

The best thing is to look for your totem animal and then speak with him. He will tell you about his own characteristics and how you can adapt them and apply them in your everyday life.

This guide is an ally, not a servant; you must maintain a attitude of respect towards him.

Your animal guide will not solve your problems; he might even, once in a while, play the opposite role by placing you in front of problems which you weren't even aware of. This is the first step along the path of the Shaman...

MONTH OF BIRTH AND TOTEM

Generally and traditionnally, the search for one's totem animal is a very personal endeavour, which involves a mystical quest including a vision, a meditation or a dream.

Nevertheless, everyone does not necessarily feel like setting out on this type of research. It takes time and perseverance, and often takes a whole lifetime.

For those who would like to be associated to a totem animal in a more general way, here are the totem animals who rule over each month of the year.

We also include characteristics which are associated to the animal as well as to the people who were born during that month.

Once you know your animal, nothing prevents you from asking for his help and guidance.

There are not fixed rules; you may have affinities with another animal than the one ruling over the month when you were born.

This general choice of a totemic animal is more a matter of affinity than anything else.

The quest and discovery of one's personal totem can begin by a very simple exploration of the affinities which one finds in general and which can serve as a starting point for a more serious Shamanic quest.

January:

White goose

- These are determined, often stubborn people, who have a piercing eye for details.

  They are visionaries in their field of activity.

February:

Otter

- They like friendly gatherings, and parties.

  They enjoy being in groups and often dislike being alone.

  They also have great vitality.

March:

Cougar

- They are often shy and withdrawn.

  They sometimes hide their talents from others.

  They prefer anonymity and often solitude.

APRIL :

HAWK

- These are beings that are concerned by others, who want to help others.

  Their frankness and honesty are often disarming.

MAY :

CASTOR

- Their loyalty is unshakeable and they do not like changes, except when it brings them more security.

  They are pacifists.

JUNE :

ROE DEER

- They are curious and often highly intelligent.

  Their nature is active, although they sometimes get anxious over nothing.

July :

Eel

- Highly sensitive, they prefer not to move.

  However, in case of danger, they are ready to do anything in order to defend their family and assets.

August :

Sturgeon

- They love being in the first place.

  They have a very generous and charming nature; they are loyal in a very restrained circle of friends and family.

September :

Bear

- Often vegetarian, they are obsessed by details.

  They are loyal and although they make friends easily, they keep their distance.

OCTOBER :

CROW

- First class communicators, they have a curious nature and are constantly seeking relations between themselves and the world.

NOVEMBER :

SNAKE

- They have a powerful nature and an intelligence based on cunning.

  They can also be vindicative when pushed to the extreme.

  They do not forget.

DÉCEMBER :

MOOSE

- They are quite fond of the wilderness and of wide open spaces.

  They have a noble and sweet nature, although they are aften quite proud.

SECOND STEP:
The Cycles of Destruction and Creation

Any Shaman knows the cycle of life and knows quite well that before creating anything, it is necessary to make room. In fact, destruction is often necessary. It is from the energy of this destruction that a new form, more appropriate to your needs, can be born. To make room for the Shamanic principles, you must destroy the principles which prevent you from perceiving the universe of a Shaman.

A Shaman feels at ease with the concept of destruction: he understands that, without it, he could not create anything new. The point is not pointless or cruel destruction, but rather being as a phenix who perishes in the flames to be reborn, later on, from his own ashes. This is similar to the destruction of an unhealthy building which must leave room for a new dwelling, more conducive to life.

This type of action and this outloook on reality is that of nature itself, and of the cycle of seasons. The fall sweeps away the summer's sweet warmth and causes the death of plants, whose fruits nourish us during the dead season. Winter litterally kills grass, the weakest insects and animals, from one season to the next; each implies the end of a state and the birth of another. Nature may sometimes seem cruel, but there is always a rebound, of a continuous cycle which perpetuates itself unrelentingly.

In our modern world, we have become obsessed with the idea of permanence, of immortality, of eternal youth. We want to have it all and not have to pay the price. The Shaman knows that, to instill new principles, he must first and foremost get rid of the old ones.

We will see further on, when we deal with traditions, the importance of initiation, which constitutes in several Shamanic cultures the Initiate's death and his rebirth.

In several ancient cultures, the applicant had to let himself be buried for a period of twenty-four to seventy-two hours.

Egyptian, aspiring initiates had to remain in a stone sarcophagus for three full days.

Other traditions have the person take drugs that simulate death and keep them in state of transe for several hours.

Others still do the same thing in a more symbolic way, by isolating the applicant or applicants in a special place where they do not see anyone for several days.

Whatever the method, it is essential to give one's life symbolically in order to be reborn into a new form.

Symbolic initiation

We hae prepared for you an initiation exercise where, symbolically, you will shed your own body: you will die to be reborn to the life of a Shaman.

This exercise makes you descend into hells, into the kingdom of Shamanic initiation.

We advise you to ask for the help of your totem animal before undertaking this initiate meditation.

Settle comfortably; as a matter of fact, it is preferable to lie down.

- Make sure you will not be disturbed for a sufficiently long period of time.

  Relax completely, breathe slowly and deeply until feeling completely relaxed.

  When you feel ready, return to the place where you met yopur totem animal. You must tell him about your desire to be initiated. Listen closely to his reply.

Your guide might refuse to bring you to the place of initiation.

- If such is the case, ask him why.

  If the answer is negative, cease immediately.

  You can re-enter the process some time later on.

If your guide gives you a green light, do as follows:

- Let him take you to the place of initiation; avoid any preconceived ideas. This place could look like anything: a cave, a white room or the inside of an ancient temple. You will receive precise instructions on the part of your guide and of the other guards, present on location.

You must now come out of your body and look at it objectively.

- With your spirit, you must destroy your body's representation: first the flesh, then the organs, and finally, the skeleton. Then, place all of these parts on a funeral pyre, and light it up in order to destroy all of your ancient body's particles.

As soon as your body is entirely reduced to ashes, lead your spirit into these ashes and completely reconstitute it.

- Inject the breath of your new existence into your ashes and, slowly, rebuild your own body.

Once this has been done, turn towards your guide and thank him for his help.

- You are now ready to leave the place of initiation and to return to the physical world. You have been through death and experienced rebirth from your own ashes, in the same way as a phenix. You are now ready to follow the path of a Shaman.

The destruction of your useless goods

You must now learn how to use the cycles of destruction and creation in your material life.

The first exercise consists in getting rid of the objects that clutter your life, which do not have their place anymore in your life.

This is crucial in order to enable you to acquire new possessions which will be more in accordance with your new lifestyle.

Remember: before creating, one must destroy.

This exercise is symbolic of the room you make in your mind for new knowledge. You may decide to keep everything, but do you have enough space for your new acquisitions?

Here is how, for example, you might proceed with your clothes.

You could then apply the technique to all of the rooms in your house.

Go to your wardrobe and office, and get rid of the articles and clothes which you did not use for more than one year.

- You can also part with all of the clothes you do not like anymore. Examine closely your needs, and decide what you want to keep.

  Give thanks to each piece of clothing or object for their usefulness and let them go mentally.

  Bring them to a charity organization so they can be of use to other people.

Do the same thing for each room in your home.

- Go through all of your possessions and get rid of all of the items that have become useless. If possible, make sure that these objects can be used second-hand.

In doing this exercise, you are preparing your indoors so they may be transformed; you are allowing space for universal energy to materialize new objects which will serve you in your new life.

Symbolically and physically, you are making room for change.

You are now ready to receive gifts from the universe and you have space to build your new existence.

The destruction and reconstruction
of your belief system

This is a very important step, since it is the ultimate foundation of what you are.

In the same way as you have made room physically in your life, you have to make room in your head.

This includes all of the habitual ways of thinking that do not serve you anymore, all of the preconceived ideas about what you are capable or incapable of doing.

You must open up your horizons and pave the way. This might seem easy to you... don't be so sure!

Often, we happen to identify with our beliefs; in a way, we have the impression that they are a part of us. This kind of belief is at the origin of many wars... Taks stock of all of the conflicts of ideology or religion which originated in differing beliefs.

You are now going to have the opportunity to go further by examining systematically all of your beliefs and by discovering to what extent you are identifying yourself to them.

You are going to discover that much courage is needed to distance yourself from them.

Remember that your beliefs can be a part of your way of thinking, but that they are not you.

What can help you, is to remember the beliefs which you had as a child and which you do not hold anymore. You might have believed in Santa Claus at some time for example.

In the same way that you have put aside this belief without destroying yourself, you can get rid of outdated beliefs.

When you change your beliefs, you do not loose your basic integrity nor your identity.

This is how you could proceed to get rid of your old beliefs.

• Firstly, sit down and make a list of all of the things and ideas in which you believe.

Create several lists, for example: one of all of your beliefs about men, another about women, another about work, money, possessions, and so on and so forth. You see, it's intricate work.

As you progress along this path, you will feel relieved, but it is also possible for you to feel a bit anxious.

Do not worry, this exercise is worth it, if only to understand what are the beliefs or ideas that hold you in place.

Then look at one of the lists and write its opposite.

- You might feel a bit queezy, but that will give you agood idea about how you you think. In the beginning, you will feel like a liar, but do not forget that, from a Shamanic perspective, the beliefs that you maintain enable you to receive from the universe.

The Shaman might be perceived as a liar, but what must be understood is that, often, the body and the subconscious need to be calmed, soothed and cajoled to change perspective. Here is an example of what we mean:

Old belief:
- Only liars manage to reach success in life.

Its opposite:
- Honesty enables me to reach success.

Old belief:
- There is not enough time for me to do everything I would like to.

Its opposite:
- I have all of the time needed to accomplish what I want.

Old belief:
- I never have enough money.

Its opposite:
- I always have enough money to satisfy my needs.

Do you understand? It might take time, but it's well worth the effort. Each old belief will be replaced by a new one.

When you will have finished, burn your lists after having torn them apart.

When an old belief re-emerges, immediately think of its opposite as being the truth.

With practice, you will end up believing in your new ideas and getting rid of your useless beliefs successfully.

The destruction of bad habits

Now, it is time to go on to another very serious step, that of destroying your bad habits, the models which you adopted automatically.

It must be kept in mind that habits should make life easier for you. Bad habits, though, are destructive and do not bring about any comfort; often, those habits that seem to make life easier do not really do that.

You may find yourself so deeply immersed in your habits that the least change can seem impossible to you. Habits which had seemed good at the beginning, have turned into a ball and chain preventing you from moving forward.

Break the circle of your habits, which, often, become superstitions.

Later on, you will succeed in getting rid of more harmful habits, because you will not feel forced to perpetuate the model.

If you wish to pursue along the Shamanic path, you should be open and ready for anything.

It is difficult to be ready if you have to follow a television show or go to bed at a set time.

So therefore examine your habits in a meticulous way and look for a different way of doing things, without changing too radically.

Here are the types of habits that hamper your progress along the Shamanic path.

There's nothing frightening about them; they're simply actions which you habitually repeat, day after day, until it becomes impossible for you to imagine any other way of going about life.

- Always following the same route to go to work, run errands, or go to school.

- Always having the same food and drink for breakfast.

- Going to bed and getting up at precisely the same time, every day.

- Wearing the same clothes day after day.

- Using the same figures of speech, the same expressions.

- Constantly coughing before speaking - or instead of speaking.

- Drinking every night, going to the same bar.

- Smoking.

- Always eating in the same restaurant or shopping at the same places.

- Always going out with the same crowd.

- Reading the newspaper every day, always reading the same newspaper.

- Always considering the world along the same perspective.

- Watching the same television shows every week.

- Getting lost in a crowd in order to avoid feeling lonely.

- Avoiding to meet people.

- Avoiding elderly people, or handicapped persons.

- Avoiding any interaction with children.

If you recognize any of these types of habits in your own life, find out how you could change them. Learn to do things differently and keep your sense of humour !

The Middle Path: Striking a Balance

Most people consider that they have either too much or too little of one of the seven following items:

- Money;

- Possessions;

- Health;

- Beauty and physical appearance;

- Relationships;

- Sex;

- Time.

Few are those who are satisfied with each of these items. Here are some examples:

- When there is too little money, feelings of being deprived crop up. However, when there is too much money, the person has a hard time managing it, which prevents them from fully enjoying life.

- The life of certain people is too cluttered, which stiffles them, whereas others do not have enough to satisfy their own needs.

- As far as health is concerned, no one can avoid allergies or colds; even those who are healthy think that this cannot last.

- Very few people are entirely satisfied with their appearance.

- When we have too few relationships, we feel isolated; when we have too many, we lose sight of who we are. Not to mention the number of unhappy relationships.

- Sexual relations are mostly unsatisfying because either they do not last or because their lack is a problem.

- Some people have too much time and get bored; others because they do not have enough, and anxiety sets in.

To try and find some balance, start by making three lists.

- In the first list, include all of the ways in which you feel disempowered, for a given element.

- In the second list, write down how you could feel uncomfortable if you had too much of that element.

- In the third list, express what state of balance would suit you for each of these elements.

Then examine your lists in order to find out which element is most lacking for you, the one for which you feel most unbalanced.

- Do a meditation during which you will ask your totem guide to help you find a state of balance in the element where you feel disempowered.

For the elements where you have too much, use the exercise in which you get rid of excess baggage.

The complete cycle... in summary

1 – Get rid of useless beliefs, of excess goods, of harmful habits and of relationships that stiffle you.

2 – Be aware that you can count on the help of your totem animal in tight situations.

3 – Get rid of your arrogance, of your false humility and guilt, in order to achieve your goals in life.

4 – Increase your ability to acquire power.

5 – Learn how to share your satisfaction and your happiness with the people around you.

6 – Learn how to receive with gratefulness.

7 – Be capable of playing a significant part in the lives of others.

Chapter 4

Native American Shamanic Practices and Rituals

T is both easy and fun to become familiar with the Shamanic universe through some of its most accessible traditions. This is a pleasant way to enrich your own culture and to slowly open up your perceptions. Shamanism must not become a chore. Even if you decide not to follow the behavior guidelines of a Shaman, you can still take advantage of certain rituals which are beneficial. However, if you do decide to follow the Shamanic path, these exercises will help to open up your perspectives and to go further in your practice.

A Gift from Heaven

For Native Americans, feathers represent a gift from the Great Spirit as well as from the bird itself, who offers part of his essence through the giving of a feather. These are mainly feathers found on the ground, in trees, left behinD by birds, for instance during their moulting phase. Shamans do not hunt down birds to get their feathers; indeed, the latter needs to be a gift offered by a bird or by another person.

The healing powers of feathers have been recoginzed for a very long time by the Native Americans as well as by other peoples.

Feathers can be found in amulets, magic bags; they are an integral part of Shamanic life.

Shamans use them as a point of convergence to allow energy to penetrate into the patient, during healing rituals.

Feathers are also used to receive and redistribute various beneficial energies.

Here are some properties related to our ally friends as well as to their finery.

EAGLE

Its feathers have a particular status in Native American magical and religious practices. They represent the sacred essence of all birds. They symbolize peace; they are also used during healing rituals, especially to disperse harmful energies and to attract beneficial energies into the patient's body. Moreover, eagle's feathers carry off our thoughts and prayers, enabling them to soar towards the Great Spirit.

DUCK

Its feathers symbolize the transition to adulthood, when one becomes capable of finding one's way. They are used during initiation ceremonies, whether to indicate the transition from adolescence to adulthood or during Shamanic initiations.

HUMMINGBIRD

Its feathers are renowned for bringing beauty and joy. They symbolize swiftness of action and gracious movements. They are particularly popular with tribes living in the Southwestern part of the US.

DOVE

Its feathers are used for rituals of peace. They play an important part during peace negotiations, and are often attached to the peace pipe.

ROOSTER

Its feathers are reserved for Shamanic warriors; they symbolize courage and the victory of day over night.

CROW

Its feathers symbolize mourning; they are used during funeral ceremonies. The Lakota Sioux pray with crow feathers for four days, at the time of death. They are only used for that purpose and are kept in a sacred place.

SWAN

Its feathers symbolize grace, beauty and kindness. For the Creeks, they represent union and marriage, and are sought after for weddings and fertility rituals. They are most often used by Medicine Women-Shamans.

HAWK

Its feathers are used to make diagnostics of bodily illnesses more accurate and specific. They are renowned, among Shamans, for their help in increasing understanding of illnesses and the knowledge of medical people.

BLUE JAY

Its feathers bring the clarity of daylight into dark or troubled situations. They let the sunshine in, thus breaking up the clouds of depression and sadness.

WHITE GOOSE

This bird marks both the beginning and the end of summer. The white goose is a great migrator; its feathers are used by Northern peoples for healing ceremonies. They also represent the mark of a Shaman for several tribes.

WATER BIRDS

The feathers of these birds have a dual symbolic function, being as much related to air as to water. They offer double protection to the Shamans who possess them, and are powerful ritual instruments. In the same way as eagle feathers, the feathers of these birds carry off our thoughts and prayers towards the Great Spirit, through the paths of streams and rivers.

NIGHT BIRDS
(OWLS)

Their feathers are used during esoteric rituals involving the use of secret knowledge. All Shamans have them, in order to invoke the guardians of sacred knowledge.

PARROT

Its feathers are rare and highly-coveted in order to decorate costumes for ritual dances and ceremonies. Because this bird can learn any language, its feathers symbolize communication, facilitating communication and translation between tribes. Its lively colors – red, green, blue and yellow – are used to recreate the rainbow, symbol of peace and prosperity among the Lakota Sioux.

MAGPIE

Its feathers are used for healing rituals. Being a vulture, the magpie helps to clean up the environment. This is why its feathers are used to clean and purify disease-stricken bodies. In the Lakota culture, the black and white feathers at the end of the magpie's wings represent a young Native maiden with jet-black hair, wearing a white gown.

HEN

Its feathers are used for the construction of a new house or among migrant peoples.

They are transported and are part of the very structure of temporary home.

The Shaman distributes them to each family, because those feathers are guarantee of an harmonious and comfortable home.

ROAD RUNNER

Everyone knows this bird through Bugs Bunny and his adventures with the coyote.

Nevertheless, this bird endemic to the American desert does exist and his speed is legendary.

Its feathers symbolize the coyote's chaotic and unpredictable energy, the coyote being a trickster par excellence.

They are also useful in increasing the natural skill of the practitioner or Shaman in magic, as well as his intuition.

NIGHTINGALE

Its feathers are endowed with a very powerful mystical significance. They help understand the complexity of rituals and assimilate knowledge of sacred things.

ROBIN

Since this is one of the first birds to return at springtime, its feathers bring renewal and are particularly valued for rituals of fertility.

Finding a Robin's feather on the ground is sign of a novel.

SCISSORTAIL

Its feathers are used to honor mothers in all Native American nations.

They are quite highly valued to point to the sun and to the four cardinal directions during ceremonies.

The Medicine Wheel

This is one of the most powerful and most widely known symbols in Native American culture.

This wheel, which represents the cycle of existence, is also found in other cultures, as the wheel of karma or chakras, which are small wheels of energy in our body.

The Medicine Wheel represents the human being and his family environment, the animals, plants and minerals living there, his house, and his nation.

How to build your own wheel

The most simple wheels are built with stones, ordinary rocks, which you can find anywhere or even buy at a tree-nuresery.

To create your wheel, you need thirty-two stones:
- A large one,
- Nineteen medium-sized ones,
- And twelve small ones.

It is preferable to make your medicine wheel outside of your home.

The wheel is ruled by the four great powers, the four directions, the four cardinal points.

- **First comes the North.** This is the direction of knowledge and wisdom; its color is white and its totem animal, the buffalo.

- **Then comes the South.** This is the direction of innocence and purity; its color is green and its totem animal, the mouse (or the hare).

- **Then comes the West.** This is the direction of introspection and inner vision; its color is black and its totem animal, the bear.

- **Then comes the East.** This is the direction of enlightenment, of understanding; its color is yellow and its totem animal, the eagle.

We are now ready to make our wheel.

- The large stone represents the Earth. Pmlace it at the center of the circle which you plan to realize.

- Surrround it then by seven medium-sized stones, which symbolize the four elements (water, earth, fire and air) and the three Guardian Spirits: Mother Earth, Grandmother Moon and Father Sky.

- Then choose four medium-sized stones who will be the Guardian spirits of the four directions. To help you recognize them later on, you can place a color spot on each of them: to the North, white; to the South, green; to the West, black; to the East, yellow. These four stones form the outer rim of your circle. They will help guide you throughout your ceremony.

- Place two medium-sized stones between each of the four cardinal point stones, so that the twelve meidum-sized stones form a circle representing the twelve moons of the medicine wheel.

- Finally, set your small stones to trace a cross : four rays leaving the center towards each of the cardinal points.

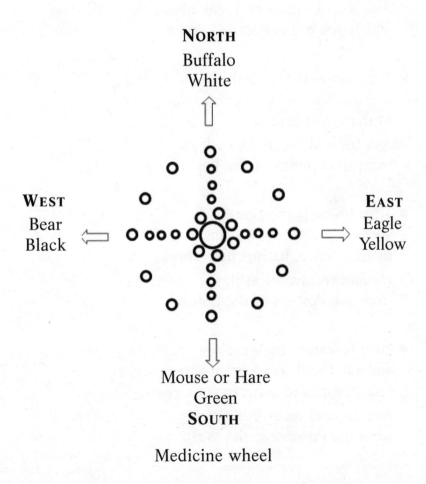

NORTH
Buffalo
White

WEST
Bear
Black

EAST
Eagle
Yellow

Mouse or Hare
Green
SOUTH

Medicine wheel

How to use the Wheel

- Light up sage or cedar incense
  (or a blend of both)
  and send the smoke first towards yourself,
  then towards the wheel.

- Ask the Great Spirit to guide you
  and to share his wisdom with you.
  Ask you question or speak about the topic
  which you are concerned about.

- Turn towards the East
  and ask the Eagle to carry your prayers
  to the Great Spirit.
  Ask for and receive blessings
  from the Powers of the East.

- Turn towards the South
  and ask the Mouse to lend you
  its innocence, its ingenuousness.
  for and receive blessings
  from the Powers of the South.

- Turn towards the West
  and ask the Bear to grant you courage
  and strength to achieve your goals.
  Ask for and receive blessings
  from the Powers of the West.

- Now place yourself to the North
  and ask the buffalo to grant you wisdom
  to understand and apply the knowledge
  which you have acuired from the totem animals,
  the Eagle, the Mouse and the Bear.
  Ask for and receive the blessings
  from the Powers of the North.

- Now look at the stone located
  at the center of the Wheel:
  It represents the Earth.
  Caress it and feel the protection
  from the Spirits of the Earth.
  Feel in the deepest core of yourself
  the bond that unites you to that stone
  which symbolizes what you are.

- Then give your thanks
  to each direction as well as to the elements
  and to the Guardian Spirits.

Native American Style
Shamanic Incense

Native Americans use herbs for purification and prayer. They believe that their prayers, thanks and acknowledgements will be guided towards the Great Spirit by the incense smoke.

Choice incense types are:

- Sage,
- Cedar,
- Sweetgrass.

Cedar is good for driving away the bad dreams. Burn it near your bed and the nightmare will not come back. If your children are sick, victims of difficult sleep or bad dreams, burn some cedar and send the smoke on their body. This smoke has the reputation to accelerate recovery, drive out bad dreams and favour good sleep.

Sage is an agent of protection and purification. It breaks up negative energies. It can also be used to greet a new day.

A combination of sage, cedar and sweetgrass is appropriate if someone dies or in the event of a tragedy.

You can easily find incense sticks from these herbs in various natural food or New Age stores.

They are made up of sage leaves, small cedar twigs and sweetgrass, rolled together and tied with thread or a thin string.

They are burnt in the same way as ordinary incense.

They are perfectly acceptable in an urban environment, where you do not have access to a forest or to trees.

However, if you want to pick your plants yourself, they will have an increased power, not with respect to the ingredients themselves, but for the benefit of your own spirit, being closer to nature.

It is a way to choose a path and to respect its precepts.

Picking your plants in the traditional way

Find your tree or your plant and sit down on the ground.

- Relax, take the time to breathe and to look around you.

  Speak to the plant, tell it what type of use you need it for: the practise of a ritual or purification, warding off bad dreams, helping others, etc.

  Explain your goals, your intentions.

  Clarify your thoughts.

  You can speak out loud or only think; but make the effort to speak to the plant itself.

Cut or pick your plant and leave something behind in exchange.

- This is an essential part of the ritual. You must leave an offering in sign of respect and gratitude towards the spirit of the plant.

  The traditional gift consists in one or two pinches of tobacco, but you can leave a coin, a few grains of corn or bread crumbs.

  Please note, the idea here is picking one or two plants, or cutting a branch from a cedar tree, not stocking up on supplies for the whole year.

  Let your plants dry for several days, in a dark and well ventilated place.

Purification and Blessing Ceremony
(smudge blessing)

For this ceremony, you must have some sage or cedar, a small container to burn herbs in (traditionally, an abalone shell is used) as well as a feather.

- Place your sage in the container and burn it.

- Offer up the smoke unto the six sacred directions.

With your feather, send the soke upwards:
- Father Sky.

Now send the smoke downwards towards the ground:
- Mother Earth.

Send the smoke Eastwards:
- The Eagle will facilitate the travel of our prayers towards the Great Spirit.

Send the smoke Westwards:
- The Bear will give you strength and stability.

Send the smoke Northwards:
- The buffalo will grant you wisdon and knowledge.

Send the smoke Southwards:
- The mouse will provide you with the innocence and ease to receive the blessings.

At the same time, you should pray:

- Ask in your own words what you would like to obtain and thank the Great Spirit for what you already have.

  You can make practical requests or, if you do not have any, simply speak about what you are feeling.

Turn Eastwards and, with your feather still, bring the smoke towards your own body:

- Starting from the feet (the Earth).

- Then to go on to the head (the sky).

- When the smoke reaches your chest and your head, ask for purity of heart and spirit.

You are now ready to carry out the ritual for another person.

- Place the person to the East and send the smoke towards her, starting by her feet and going up to her head.

- Start by the front of the body and make the participant turn to send the smoke to her back.

- If you have to do this for a bedridden person, start by their feet and finish with their head.

- You can insist on the diseased part where the illness is focused.

A good piece of advice:

- Disactivate your smoke detectors when you are carrying out this ritual. It is particularly unpleasant to have them ring out in the middle of a ceremony.

  Once the ritual is over, let some sage burn in the shell.

  Then, throw out the ashes, either outside or in the toilet water, so they can return to a natural environment.

Ritual Sauna
(sweat lodge)

Here is an example of a Shamanic ritual which you can easily recreate in the countryside or even in your backyard. The rules are easy to follow, among which certain precautions which it is essential to take.

Everyone has heard about the sweatlodge ceremonies, which are ritual purification ceremonies. They are common to most Native American tribes and used on many different occasions.

This is a physical and spiritual purification ritual. In the Native American tradition, along with sweat, toxins and illnesses are expelled. This sweating process has the additional advantage of soothing the mind and enabling the conscious to reconnect with more spiritual realities. This ritual is often carried out before other ceremmonies, which require thorough purification.

For a Shaman or an apprentice Shaman, it is a ritual to obtain a vision.

This is the foundation of any Shamanic work, since the Shaman relies on his visions, his intuitions, to guide his existence.

Native Americans believe that the combination of the elements of fire, water and earth help to give participants a more intimate knowledge of the Earth, of themselves, of animals, and of all of creation.

How to practise this ritual

Organizing this ritual is quite simple.

- It requires a sufficiently large space outside, in a place where you can light up a fire to heat up stones.

Traditionally, tree branches had to be cut and buffalo skins or covers had to be spread on the structure.

- In our times, a tent canvas is enough, without floor, large enough to contain the number of people expected to attend.

Before setting up the tent, you have to dig a hole in its center, in which you will drop the white-hot stones.

- At the bottom of this hole, you put sage and cedar which, heated up, wil give off a fragrant smoke conducive to meditation.

Not too far away from the tent, the fire guardian (a crucial position) heats up the stones:

- Volcanic rocks are recommended.
- During that time, you raise the tent.

Once everything is ready:

- The sweatlodge leader invites the participants to come into the tent, one by one, and to sit on the ground. This is done in silence.

Once everyone has taken place:

- The fire guardian arrives with the white-hot rocks.

- He sets them down into the hole garnished with herbs.

- He gives pitchers of water to the leader and leaves, closing the tent door behind him.

- The smoke, and the smell of the herbs and the hot rocks can be felt.

- The time has now come to produce steam. The sweatlodge leader pours some water over the rocks. The purifying steam rises up, as well as the temperature.

This is a time of contemplation and meditation.

- The amount of time spent inside is to be decided by the sweatlodge leader.

- When he gives the signal, the ceremony ends and the participants file out one by one.

This is an unforgettable experience of contemplation and peace.

A few rules

There is always a sweatlodge leader.

- This is a very important, even vital position. Make sure your leader is experienced, that he has taken part in many rituals of this kind. He is the one in charge of your security.

The fire guardian is co-leader.

- He takes care of feeding the fire, bringing the stones, closing off thev tent and bringing water or any other necesary object. If there is any music, he is in charge of the magnetic tapes. It is not a good idea to expose a tape player to the steam or to the extreme heat inside the tent. He also has to maintain calm and hramony outside the the tent. This is sometimes a difficult task, as the non-participants do not always understand that it is not appropriate to shout or to speak in a loud voice in the surroundings.

There is a very strict rule for women.

- This is not a question of sexism, but of power. Women are not allowed to take part in this ritual when they have their period. It is not because they are considered impure, on the contrary. For Native Americans, the period of menstruations is when they are the most powerful; it would therefore be ridiculous to weaken this power by a ritual of this kind. There are other, more appropriate rituals for women during this period.

Wear light, comfortable and decent clothes.

- Yous spiritual experience will be that more beneficial from it.

Do not take any alcohol or drugs twenty four hours before and after the ritual.

- Give your body the chance to take advantage of this purification.

Be respectful of those who are leading this ritual.

- Do not make their task more difficult than it is. This is not the right time to tell jokes or to joke around.

Do not take any alcohol, drugs or food during the ritual.

- Drugs can be particularly dangerous during this type of ritual. Forget what you might have read in certain books, reality could lead you straight to a hospital.

If you feel bad during the ritual.

- If you cannot stand the heat and the smoke, make a sign to the sweatlodge leader and leave immediately. This is not some endurance contest, you are not there to prove anything.

If you have any health problems.

- Consult your physician before taking part in this kind of ritual.

The Symbolism of Objects you Find

Button
- Happiness in your home.

Coin
- Prosperity.

Gull feather
- Freedom to do whatever you want.

Jay feather
- Opportunities.

Key
- You are going to find what you have long been looking for.

Pine cone
- Wealth to come.

Shell
- A new love.

Dream catchers

Dream catchers are common to several Native American tribes.

The Ojibwas, the Lakota Sioux, the Creeks, the Zunis, the Tinglits and even the Hopishave legends about spiders; Native American cultures in South America also have legends about the spiderwoman.

The spider is a mythical animal, with strange and mysterious powers for Native American peoples.

It weaves its web anywhere and draws marvelous patterns, worthy of the greatest masters.

Its bite does not kill; itprefers to paralyze its opponents which she later one uses as food.

Its dietary habits also feed many speculations. She does not feed off flesh but rather blood, the very substance of life.

As you can imagine that in itself has given rise to a number of additional myths.

For the Hopis, the spiderwoman is one of the powers who created the universe. Her power is greatest at night, because during that time the stars themselves are the canvas on which she weaves her web, encompassing the entire universe.

The Ojibwas say that we owe dream-catchers to Grandmother Spider. They are only, in fact the miniature models of the large web which she weaves between stars. All of the thoughts and messages from daytime are trapped in the web and are transformed into dreams. The scattering of our thoughts and messages is the reason why our dreams are often so incomprehensible and require the help of a Shaman to be decyphered.

The dream catcher is a small representation of the sky's great canvas. It is a precious gift from Grandmother Spider, since catchers serve to filter out the pieces of messages coming to us as dreams, filtering out nightmares and other bad dreams.

In all Native American cultures, the dreamcatcher is considered to be a good-luck charm; when offered by a friend, this means that he is taking our best interests into consideration. The gift of uninterrupted sleep is a precious gift indeed. The giver's energye is thus blended witgh Grandmother Spider's energy, since simply making a dreamcatcher fills it with beneficial influences.

How operates the Dream catchers

The Dream catcher is connected with his owner. When night comes, it filters out energies so that only good and useful dreams reachs the dreamer's head.

Bad dreams, nightmares, and that should disturb the sleeper, are trapped in the web of the catcher. Some cultures threads jai or onyx pearls in the web, because those stones possess properties that absorb negative influences.

When day comes, Grandfather Sun destroys negative energies with its rays, and the catcher is ready to continue doing its work the following night.

The supplies

Use a wooden ring:

- The choice of the diameter is up to you. Be careful! The smaller the ring, the simpler the model you must choose!

Traditionally, Native Americans used animal sinews to weave their dreamcatcher.

- Now, we are going to use a thread soaked in bee wax. You can also use a weaving thread, but the result will not be as solid as with the bee wax thread.

To garnish the outer rim, thin straps of deer leather were used.

- You can find some easily in specialized shops.

- You can also use ribbon or tissue.

- You can also integrate stones into your project, it's just a matter of taste.

- Traditional catchers are also adorned with feathers, the properties of which you have just read about.

How to go about it

It's simple.

- First, you have to surround your ring with a ribbon or a leather strap, in order to cover it completely. Finally, you knot your thread in the middle of the ring, then you surround the ring seven times.

- You continue and slip your thread between each thread, until reaching the center. You can string stones or pearls along your thread.

- This first pattern is a traditional Native American pattern; it's the spider's pattern. You can weave any pattern you wish into your ring, for example flowers or birds, a pentacle, or any other esoteric sign.

The Wicca
Purification Ritual

In the Shamanic universe, everything is a symbol. To mark your entrance into that universe, it is a good idea to begin by a purification ritual which symbolizes the leaving behind of your past influences, or your old perceptions.

This ritual is a symbol of your desire to start out along the Shamanic pathway.

This is a ritual of wicca origin. It is very simple and you can add all the invocations you wish to it.

We will be asking for the intercession of archangels in this ritual, because these are very strong and very luminous powers. You can substitute whomever seems right to you, depending on your personal choice.

Begin by cleaing your room or the house, very thoroughly. Once this is done, gather the following items:

- A cup or a glass which you fill with water (tap water is fine);

- A small bowl of water, made out of glass or ceramic, which you will fill with ordinary salt (not sea salt);

- A green candle in a candle holder;

- An incense stick (it is preferable to use sage, pine or cedar for this ritual).

Go to the center of the room with, at your feet, a plate containing the items listed earlier.

- Turn towards the north, holding the salt bowl with both hands, raising it towards the sky, saying:

  I invoke the presence of the Archangel Michael, guardian of the North and of the Earth element.

  O, powerful Michael, help me purify this room from any harmful influence

  And to banish any negative energies from it.

- Go around the room, turning in a clockwise direction, and throw a few salt grains in each corner of the room, saying:

  With the salt of the Earth,

  I purify this location and banish

  Any negative energies from here.

- Return to the center of the room.
  Now turn towards the West, holding the water cup and raising it to the sky, say:

  I invoke the presence of the Archangel Gabriel,

  Guardian of the West and of the water element.

  O, powerful Gabriel, help me

  purify this room from any harmful influence

  and banish any negative energies from it.

- Go around the room, turning in a clockwise direction and throwing a few drops of water in each corner of the room, say:

With the water of the Earth,
I purify this location and banish
Any negative energies from here.

- Return to the center of the room. Now turn towards the South, holding the candle and raising it to the sky, say:

I invoke the presence of the Archangel Uriel,
Guardian of the South and of the fire element.
O, powerful Uriel, help me purify this room
from any harmful influence and banish
Any negative energies from it.

- Go around the room, turning in a clockwise direction and stopping in each corner of the room, say:

With the fire of the Earth,
I purify this place and banish
Any negative energies from here.

- Return to the center of the room. Now turn towards the East, holding the lighted incense and raising it to the sky, say:

JI invoke the presence of the Archangel Raphaël,
Guardian of the West and of the air element.

O, powerful Raphaël, help me purify this room

from any harmful influence and banish
Any negative energies from here.

- Go aournd the room, turning in a clockwise direction and stopping in each corner of the room, say:

  With the air of the Earth,
  I purify this place and banish
  Any negative energies from here.

- Now take a broom and, symbolically, sweep away all negative influences from the room, saying:

  I banish all negative and harmful influences
  from my environment.

If you want to purify your home completely, repeat this ritual in every room, starting by the one furthest away from the entrance door.

- Finish by the hall and entrance door, and sweep away all negative influences outside.

Chapter 5

Tibetan Shamanic Tradition and Exercises

❧ ⸻ ❧

The Sources of Shamanism

AS we saw earlier, Shamanism has several facets. It is found in many different cultures, all over the world. Shamanism is also pre-Christian in terms of its origins, which is not to say however that it is not active in present times, nor that Christianity was successful in attempting to eradicate it.

We'll see, a bit further on, that despite efforts by missionaries, Shamanism has blossomed in the midst of societies practising slavery, in the Southof the United States, and in the Carribean Islands.

This brings us back to our original point, when we mentionned that Shamans make use of each and every circumstance, whatever that may be. Part of the Shaman's instinct is to use whatever suits him, adapting whatever comes his way to his own needs.

The best example of this practice is Voodoo. It is a combination of Nigerian Yoruba practices, brought in by the majority of slaves coming from Nigeria in the XVIIIth and XIXth centuries, combined with the new Christian practices forced on to the slaves. Voodoo is still practised nowadays under various forms; the best known forms of Voodoo come from the Island of Haïti and from the City of New Orleans, Louisiana.

There is also a very wide range of Native American Shamanic practises, as we saw earlier. However, it is interesting to notice that some practices also come from Tibet, from the Shamans that were there before the Buddhist lamas, and whose beliefs were integrated into Tibetan Buddhism. Once again, we must keep in mind that Shamans use whatever works best for them, and therefore that they do not hesitate to borrow customs and practices from other traditions, if these methods can help them achieve their goals more easily.

This should not be interpreted as a lack of respect; on the contrary, Shamans hold every belief in very high respect, since according to them, each of them have their own proper place in the universe.

Becoming a Shaman implies a very high degree of tolerance and respect for the beliefs of other people.

This does not mean that you have to follow them all, but that you should respect the freedom of choice of each individual person, their freedom to believe whatever they want to believe in.

To illustrate the differences that exist among various

Shamanic traditions, we invite you to an overview, both from a historical and from a geographical point of view.

In this chapter, we will look at the traditions of Tibet, and, in the next one, we will cover the traditions of the Navajo people, as well as Voodoo.

Some traditions have become extinct, whereas others are flourishing, despite our technological universe. But all of them have contributed and still contribute to making Shamanism what it is today, a path which you can now enter into.

We have also included some exercises which you will be able to use in your Shamanic training. It is interesting to know the origins of the exercises we offer, and the cultures which gave rise to them.

The Bön Religion...
Before Tibetan Budddhism

When we speak about the ancient traditions of Tibet, we are not speaking about Tibetan Budddhism as such, but about the Bön tradition. Buddhism set foot in Tibet only arround 600 AD. The traditions that were already there are several thousands of years old, slowly combining to become the Bön religion.

The Bön worship is relatively complex; it has a hierarchy of Shaman priests, made up of nine separate groups.

The first one gathers:

- Magician priests, who are mainly in charge of making exorcism amulets. There are, in this tradition, 360 different exorcism rituals and approximately 8,400 different ways of practising them.

The second group:

- Is recognized through the small juniper drums which they carry around. They are in charge of magical operations for success and prosperity.

The third group:

- Is made up of exorcists that confront evil in all of its forms, in order to preserve the world. They wear tiger fur hats.

The fourth group:

- Gathers priests who protect the lives of the living and of the inhabitants of the afterworld. They can prevent a soul from pursuing its journey if they consider him or her to be unworthy of doing so; they can also accelerate their movement.

The fifth group:

- Is made up of priests in charge of guarding the calendar. They decide of when feasts and celebrations are to occur. They are also in charge of erasing sins and keeping records of accumulated merits.

The sixth group:

- Is that of ascetics, who study the traditions'secret and magical doctrines.

The seventh group:

- Priests who study mantras and rule over sacrifices.

The eighth group:

- Is made up of fortune-tellers, who read into the future as well as into the past.

The ninth group:

- Is in charge of protecting the most secret doctrines in the Bön traditions.

For hundreds of years, the new religion attempted to make the Bön worship disappear, but failed in doing so. Even in present times, it is practised in the Western part of Tibet. Both traditions have also merged; they have borrowed from each other, and as you will see further on, some Bön exercises resemble Hindu exercises, and vice-versa.

Both religions have Shamans, and Shamans being what they are, they use whatever practises they have access to, regardless of their cultural origin.

This is why Tibetan Shamanic practises are so tangled up that it is almost impossible to distinguish those of Bön origin and those of Buddhist origin; especially given the fact that the latter has largely inspired itself from the traditions of India, where Buddhism originally came from.

At any rate, attempting to do so would be useless, since Shamans use whatever suits them, re-organizing, and adapting various methods, until having devised something that suits their specific needs.

Exercises

We are going to propose exercises that will allow you to increase your personal power and enter into different Shamanic universes. These exercises are similar to Buddhist traditions but they are a little different. The origin of the breathing exercises is quite nebulous. Explanations about chakras or tunnels belong to several cultures. The goal of these exercises is to increase your sense perceptions, to develop your psychic and extra-sensorial faculties, and to increase your personal power reservoir.

Breathing Exercises

Breathing is an indispensable tool for the followers of Bon Shamanism as well as those of Lamaism in the Tibetan tradition.

When we breathe, we inhale oxygen and we exhale carbon dioxide.

When a Shaman breathes, he inhales cosmic energy, an energy that he can transform easily to manifest what he wants. He exhales what he doesn't need: false beliefs, outmoded certainties. He makes room for universal energy.

Breathing becomes a physical and spiritual life exercise that allows the Shaman to become aware of the breath of life that circulates within him.

PRELIMINARY BREATHING

The goal of this exercise is to calm you down and to put you in the type of mental state necessary to meditate, to astral travel, to travel to past lives or simply to relax.

Before beginning any Shamanic practice, it is suggested that you do the exercise that is known as the nine breaths.

- 1. Breath slowly (inhale and exhale) three times through only the right nostril while turning your head slowly from right to left.

- 2. Breathe slowly (inhale and exhale) three times through only the left nostril while turning your head slowly from left to right.

- 3. Breath slowly (inhale and exhale) three times through both nostrils while projecting the breath in front of you and in keeping your head still.

- Repeat these three breathing exercises three times each; begin by breathing softly, then breathe with more and more intensity.

RYTHMICAL BREATHING

This exercise aims at regularizing your breathing and providing as much oxygen as possible throughout your meditation, your relaxation or any other Shamanic journey.

In addition, it helps to concentrate your attention on your breathing rather than on your wandering thoughts, which can interfere when you've decided to empty out your mind.

You can consider this exercise to be preliminary to any relaxation practise.

It can also be a valuable tool whenever you feel stressed. You just have to concentrate on your breathing to instantly experience a state of calm.

Begin by regularizing your breathing: this is a truly natural physical function. Concentrate on your breathing.

- Inhale and slowly count to four.

- Hold your breath and slowly count to two.

- Exhale and slowly count to four.

- Keep your lungs empty and slowly count to two.

  Repeat this rhythm until it becomes natural.

Once you have this down, increase your numbers:

- Inhale and count to six, for example, and suspend your breath for a count of three. This is not a contest to stretch your breathing. Choose a comfortable rhythm and keep it.

If this rhythm does not suit you:

- Practice the exercise until you have found the rhythm which you find to be the most pleasant for yourself.

- Once you have established your breathing rhythm, spend a few minutes – about three to five minutes – oxygenating your organism in order to quiet down the troublesome little inner voices.

The advantage of this rhythmic breathing: when your thoughts interrupt your concentration, all you have to do is to fix your attention on the rhythm of your breathing.

You can also imagine that when you exhale, you chase away any troublesome thoughts that might bother you. With a little practice, you will be able to concentrate better.

Relaxation Exercise

Relaxation is an essential exercise for any Shamanic practice. Over time you will be able to reach a state of relaxation in a few seconds, but to do so, you have to practice. Here is an exercise taken from the Lamaist tradition that works very well. It is very simple and easy to follow. You can practice it comfortably installed in an armchair, for example, or lying on your back.

Think of your feet:
- Concentrate all of your attention on this part of your body and become your feet. Move them. Tense them to tighten your muscles then let them relax completely. Repeat this action several times until there is no more tension in your feet or in your ankles.

Now think of your calves:
- Concentrate all of your attention on this part of your body and become your calves. Tense these muscles and let go of the tension. Repeat this action until you feel the muscles of your calves relax completely.

Now think of your thigh muscles:
- Concentrate all of your attention of this part of your body and become your thighs. Tense these muscles and then let go of the tension. Tense them and release the tension several times until all tension has disappeared.

Now think of your buttock muscles:

- Concentrate all of your attention of this part of your body and become your buttocks. Tighten them, and then relax them until they are completely free of tension.

Now think of your abdomen:

- This is a privileged site of tension so pay particular attention to it.

  Concentrate all of your attention of this part of your body and become your abdomen.

  Tighten the muscles of your stomach, and then let go.

  Repeat this until you feel free from all tension.

  Breath deeply. You will feel oxygen penetrating more fully the front part of your body.

Now think of your hands:

- Concentrate all of your attention of this part of your body and become your hands.

  Close your fists then slowly relax them.

  Repeat this exercise until you feel your fingers completely relax and your hands open gently.

Now think of your arms and your forearms:

- Concentrate all of your attention of this part of your body and become your arms. Tense your muscles and relax them until you feel them become heavy and completely relaxed.

Now think of your back:

- Concentrate all of your attention of this part of your body and become your back.
  Tense your muscles and relax them until you feel your back sink, like in the sand.

Now think of your chest:

- Concentrate all of your attention of this part of your body and become your chest.
  Tense these muscles and relax them several times until all tension has gone.

Now think of your shoulders:

- Concentrate all of your attention of this part of your body and become your shoulders.
  Move them, tense the muscles several times to get rid of all accumulated tension.
  Repeat this action until you feel your shoulders sink lightly, like in the sand.

Now think of your neck:

- Concentrate all of your attention of this part of your body and become your neck.
  Tense your muscles and relax them several times until all tension has gone.

Now think of your face:

- Concentrate all of your attention of this part of your body and become your face.

Tense the area around your teeth then let go.
Repeat this several times until all tension has gone.

Now think of your scalp :

- Concentrate all of your attention of this part of your body and become your scalp.
Knit your eyebrows, and then relax them to liberate the tension in your scalp.

Note :

Take enough time to really let go and relax. This exercise is excellent when you suffer from insomnia : it allows you to calm your anxiety.

Practice your rhythmic breathing while relaxing. When you feel your concentration vanish, breath deeply and count slowly, then continue your relaxation exercise.

The Chakras

The Tibetan Shamans, whether they practice Bon or Lamaism, consider that the individual receives or loses energy through the seven principal chakras. This energy has a specific frequency that corresponds to a color and a sound. This tradition seems at first sight to come from Buddhism. However, the most ancient texts lead us to believe that knowledge of the chakras or the tunnels of power existed before Buddhism and even Hinduism. The origin of the chakras is rather cloudy. However, to facilitate understanding this theory and to explain how it works, we have taken the Buddhist beliefs that are more familiar to our culture.

What is a chakra ?

Chakra is a Sanskrit term that means "wheel" or more precisely "rotating disk". In fact, a chakra is a meeting point of psychic energy canals. It is also an intersection where several levels converge. There are seven principal or major chakras, twenty-one minor chakras, several less important chakras and also energy points or acupuncture points that are really chakras as they are energy conduits. With all these entry points, our bodies resemble a sponge that absorbs energy. We are constantly bathed by invisible currents that criss-cross our environment.

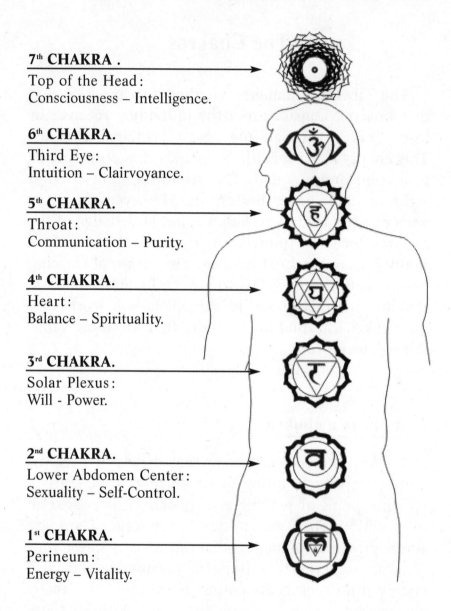

7ᵗʰ CHAKRA .
Top of the Head :
Consciousness – Intelligence.

6ᵗʰ CHAKRA.
Third Eye :
Intuition – Clairvoyance.

5ᵗʰ CHAKRA.
Throat :
Communication – Purity.

4ᵗʰ CHAKRA.
Heart :
Balance – Spirituality.

3ʳᵈ CHAKRA.
Solar Plexus :
Will - Power.

2ⁿᵈ CHAKRA.
Lower Abdomen Center :
Sexuality – Self-Control.

1ˢᵗ CHAKRA.
Perineum :
Energy – Vitality.

The Human Body's Seven Main Chakras

The Seven Main Chakras
and the Seven Etheric Bodies

Each of the main chakras corresponds to a certain level or to a specific envelope around the physical body.

For visualization, we speak about layers or levels, but all these envelopes each have a different frequency and occupy the same space in the body.

Their respective rays vary by a few centimeters from the physical body to several meters in certain cases around the body.

Contrary to what popular tradition says, the aura does not have the structure of an onion where one can peel successive layers. If one can see the levels, it is because colors exist at different vibratory levels that are visible separately.

Each of the principal chakras is attached to a specific level or to an envelope that faithfully reproduces the body and the organs as well as the other chakras.

Each of the astral bodies is linked to the others, and there is an energy exchange between the different astral levels.

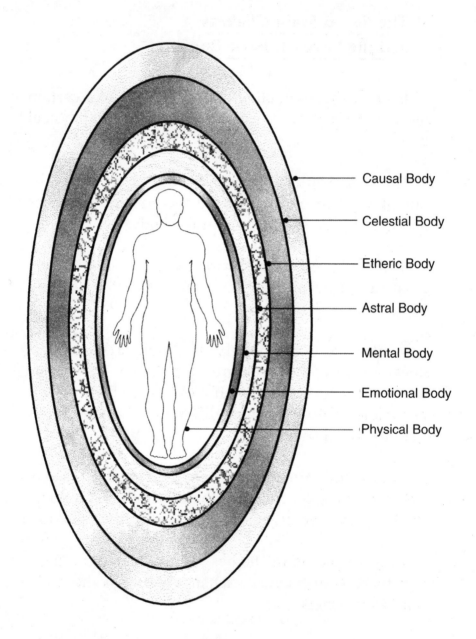

Causal Body

Celestial Body

Etheric Body

Astral Body

Mental Body

Emotional Body

Physical Body

The Seven Bodies of the Human Being
Form His Aura.

The Energetic Functions of the Chakras consist in:

- Visualizing the astral body and therefore the physical body.

- Presiding over consciousness and development of the different psychological levels.

- Transmitting energy from one astral level to the next. Each astral body, even when linked to a distinct chakra, possesses all the chakras that use a different frequency, specific to this astral level.

Here is a brief description of each of the chakras as well as their ethereal envelopes.

THE ROOT CHAKRA

- **Location:** at the bottom of the spine, about an inch from the anus;

- **Element:** Earth;

- **Function:** survival, anchor point in the physical world;

- **Glands:** adrenals;

- **Color:** red;

- **Mantra:** Lam;

- **Incense:** Cedar.

THE BASIC ETHERIC BODY

The first level is linked to the Root Chakra. This is only a rudimentary magnetic field that allows you to know instinctively that someone is coming towards you before contact.

This envelope was more present in primitive man as he was always in danger.

As the root chakra is directly linked to survival, you are award of this envelope when your defenses are activated.

This is also the first level that appears when you do exercises to see the aura. It appears as a gray shadow surrounding the body.

We can say that this envelope shows us the difference between a living and a dead body. Even if someone is immobile in a deep coma, we know that he is still alive. When someone dies, we instantly know because the subtle magnetic field is absent.

The basic ethereal body produces vital energy that is essential to our survival. It plays on the same team as the other astral envelopes to keep our bodies alive.

The genital organs chakra

- **Location**: reproductive organs level;

- **Element**: water;

- **Function**: reproduction, seat of the emotions;

- **Glands**: ovaries, testicles;

- **Color**: orange;

- **Mantra**: Vam;

- **Incense**: Gardenia.

THE EMOTIONAL BODY

The second level is the emotional body. It is linked to the sexual organs chakra.

As its name indicates, this envelope is associated with emotions.

Its structure is more fluid that the ethereal body and approximately resembles the contours of the physical body.

The body has all the colors of a rainbow and the shades can be glossy or flat, clear or cloudy, depending on the underlying emotions. The more an emotion is alive and clear, the more the colors are bright and clear. The opposite is true as the more an emotion is confused and dark, the more the colors are blurred and lifeless.

This envelope is easy enough to perceive. In fact it appears like spots of color that spurt out of the body. This is the body that people generally see as the aura. The chakras appear as circles of luminous color that reflect the gradation of a rainbow.

- **Chakra 1**: red;
- **Chakra 2**: orange;
- **Chakra 3**: yellow;
- **Chakra 4**: green;
- **Chakra 5**: blue;
- **Chakra 6**: indigo;
- **Chakra 7**: white.

THE SOLAR PLEXUS CHAKRA

- **Location:** five centimeters above the navel;

- **Element:** fire;

- **Function:** home of the will and vital energy;

- **Glands:** pancreas;

- **Color:** yellow;

- **Mantra:** Ram;

- **Incense:** cinnamon.

THE MENTAL BODY

This envelope occupies a higher frequency than the first two and its structure is associated with thinking and all mental processes.

Its color is yellow and it resembles the body contours of which it has the structure.

All of our thoughts and ideas take form at this level. They appear as more or less brilliant forms according to the clarity of the thought, the strength of an idea, or the involvement in a project. The degree of concentration also plays a role.

These "thought forms" take the color of the underlying emotions or more precisely the spots of color linked to our emotions superimpose on the forms of our ideas.

This envelope is a bit more difficult to perceive individually as it is linked essentially to a mental process.

THE HEART CHAKRA

- **Location:** between the breasts at the heart level;

- **Element:** air;

- **Function:** home of feelings, forgiveness and love. It also links the three preceding chakras to the following three chakras and permits the transformation of energy coming from one level to another;

- **Glands:** thymus;

- **Color:** green;

- **Mantra:** Laam;

- **Incense:** lavender.

THE ASTRAL BODY

This level is crucially important. It is a bridge between the three previous envelopes, related to our physical body and material reality, and the three subsequent envelopes that are mainly related to spiritual reality.

As we form a whole, it carries out a constant exchange of information and energy between the three first levels and the others.

However, there are differences between energy coming from the bodies directly linked to the material aspect of our being and levels five, six and seven.

The fourth level transforms these energies and makes them compatible with the form for which the energy is destined.

The ethereal, emotional and mental bodies produce an energy that is associated with the body and physical reality, which is more substantial that the energy produced by the following bodies such as psychic nature; both of which are incompatible.

The fourth level, because of the intervention of the heart chakra, serves as a bridge to link the material and spiritual dimensions; but its role does not stop there: the heart chakra filters energies and transforms them in a way that energy coming from the material plane can circulate on the spiritual plane and vice versa.

It is this envelope that leaves the body when we project ourselves onto the astral plane.

During an out of body experience, it is the superior levels that travel, as this envelope is linked to the physical or spiritual planes, information is retransmitted to the physical levels by the intervention of the astral body.

Even though we name this envelope "astral body", we must specify that it is made up of four envelopes that correspond toour body's four higher chakras.

The astral envelope is formless; it is composed of pink clouds punctuated with color resembling those of the emotional body but with purer tones.

The astral body is associated with feelings that are of a more or less consistent volatile nature than the emotions.

The chakras have the same range of colors here as the second level, with the exception of the heart chakra that scintillates a vibrant pink in the case of a magnetic person.

When people fall in love, one can see arcs of pink light that form between the heart chakras of the individuals.

When the relationship lasts more than a short time, other links are formed between the different chakras. The longer this relationship lasts, the more solid and numerous are the energy cords uniting the beings.

The role of the astral body is complex and essential for all physical and psychic development.

THE THROAT CHAKRA

- **Location:** in the hollow of the throat;

- **Element:** sound;

- **Function:** communication, creativity;

- **Glands:** thyroid gland;

- **Color:** blue;

- **Mantra:** Ham;

- **Incense:** oliban.

THE ETHERIC BODY MODEL

This envelope is thus named because it contains all of the elements of the physical body in a plane or model form. The body serves as a vehicle to the ethereal body at the first level, which in its turn, serves as model to the physical body. The ethereal body model contains the perfect form of our body. This level corresponds to our physical body on the spiritual plane. The energy that it projects permits our body to operate at an optimum.

To maintain our physical existence, we need the energy of the ethereal body from the first level as well as that of the ethereal body model at the fifth level. The problem resides in the nature of the energy or in the quality of it. The energy at the first level comes from elements directly linked to the material and physical world: all the bad, all the imperfections that afflict our body transpose onto our ethereal body.

It is not the same for the ethereal body model that preserves our body plane. Here we can understand the importance of the heart chakra in its energy transformation work. When the energy at the first level reaches the heart chakra, it sends a message to the fifth level that can reply by sending the necessary energy for the rebuilding of the physical body. This spiritual energy contains healing elements for the body, passes by the heart chakra that adapts it to the frequency of the ethereal body. The exchange can happened thanks to the bridge formed by the fourth chakra.

160

THE THIRD EYE CHAKRA

- **Location:** between the eyebrows, a little above the eyes;

- **Element:** light;

- **Function:** intuition and all of the psychic and extra-sensorial faculties;

- **Glands:** pineal;

- **Color:** purple;

- **Mantra:** Om;

- **Incense:** acacia.

THE CELESTIAL BODY

The Celestial Body is an opalescent luminous envelope, a little like mother-of-pearl, with gold and silver reflections. This body can seem shapeless because of its luminosity and its pastel color rays that fuse in its center.

This level corresponds to spiritual emotions: we can access mystical ecstasy here, where the being understands that he is one with the universe.

All religious mystical experiences are felt at this level.

When a being reaches this level of consciousness with the help of mediation and other exercises, he perceives that light and love exists in everything. Impregnated with light, he feels the ultimate fusion with God.

At this moment a canal opens between his heart chakra and his celestial chakra, where a stream of unconditional love floats.

This connection between the two chakras allows the combination of love that we feel for other beings and the universe, and the mystical ecstasy flowing from spiritual love to transcend material reality. Unconditional love is born from this union.

THE CROWN CHAKRA

- **Location:** on top of the head;

- **Element:** thinking;

- **Function:** understanding, anchor point with the universe;

- **Glands:** pituitary;

- **Color:** mauve;

- **Mantra:** OM;

- **Incense:** lotus.

THE CAUSAL BODY

This body appears in the form of an egg of golden light that includes all of the other astral envelopes.

This is a complex level where all information about our life plan, our previous incarnations, our limitations and our restrictions, things that we have to settle during our present incarnation and so on.

In brief, this envelope contains everything that we are and that we have been.

It is also our principal source of energy that takes the form of a golden current that circles from above to below along our spinal column.

In the middle of the egg, one can see the form of a golden body with all its chakras faithfully reproducing our physical body form.

This is the last level directly linked to our present incarnation.

Exercise to energize the chakras and increase the interaction between the ethereal and physical bodies.

Lie down or position yourself comfortably and take care not to be disturbed.

- This exercise aims to energize each of your chakras and to increase your level of physical energy.

- Begin by a relaxation or at least a breathing exercise.

- *I think of the color red and when I feel its ray come into my body, I relax.*

  The color red enters my root chakra and I feel the Earth energy enter into me.

  I feel well and completely relaxed by the beneficial effect of this luminous ray.

  I completely relax thanks to the color red.

- *I now think of the color orange and when I feel its ray come into my body, I relax.*

  The orange color enters into my genital organs chakra and right away I feel my emotions calm down. They become harmonized and flow through me like a wave, slowly leaving me. I feel completely calm because of the refreshing action of this orange ray. I completely relax thanks to the color orange.

• *I now think of the color yellow and when I feel its ray come into my body, I relax.*

The color yellow enters into my solar plexus chakra and I feel, that all efforts that I have put into unsuccessful attempts, cease to drain my energy and will.

With the beneficial actions of the yellow ray, I can align my will and devote my energy towards beneficial pursuits for myself and those around me.

I completely relax thanks to the color yellow.

• *I now think of the color green and when I feel its ray come into my body, I relax.*

The color green enters my heart chakra and I feel that all of the feelings that I have experienced for myself, others and the universe have been refreshed and purified due to the beneficial action of this ray.

• *I take a few seconds to forgive those who have done me wrong, consciously or not, and I liberate all karmic debt that concerns me.*

I also pardon the wrong that I might have caused others, consciously or not, as well as what I have caused to myself. I completely relax thanks to the color green.

- *I now think of the color blue and when I feel its ray come into my body, I relax.*

The color blue enters into my throat chakra and all the words that I have said, or not, all the words that have stayed blocked in my throat are liberate harmoniously under the beneficial influence of this ray.

The color blue cleans my communication channels that are now free and open, permitting me to communicate with the astral entities.

I relax completely thanks to the color blue.

- *I now think of the color purple and when I feel its ray come into my body, I relax.*

The color purple enters into my third eye chakra and I feel my psychic centers with the beneficial action of this ray.

Little by little, I feel my extra sensorial faculties develop and I acquire new knowledge.

I relax completely thanks to the color purple.

- *I now think of the color mauve and when I feel its ray come into my body, I relax.*

The color mauve enters into my crown chakra and I feel the energy of the universe enter into me. Under the beneficial influence of this ray, I feel that I have a place in the universe, that I have a role to play on this earth. I completely relax thanks to the color mauve.

- *I take the time to feel the harmony of these colors and the energies that flow through me. I feel well.*

Note:

You can also work on your chakras individually by visualizing the chakra in question and by receiving the energy of the corresponding color.

You can also repeat the mantra linked to each of the chakras to improve your concentration or to increase the vibratory level of your body.

Another Perspective on Chakras:
Tunnels of Power

In the Bon tradition, the chakras are the reservoirs of elements and information that are often presented in the form of memories, ancestral memories, fears, blockages, skills, talents and emotions, etc.

Each of these chakras is both a reservoir and an opening. When you decide to travel in these tunnels, to explore them, and to visit their universes, this reaffirms your adherence to the Shamanic path.

Each tunnel is also an opening into a particular universe or rather a different facet of the beyond.

You can find the solution to problems, visit your past lives and acquire new knowledge and new talents through these openings.

These tunnels offer you an exceptional opportunity to study and to discover your own symbolism, your personal power, and your place in the universe. This is quite a fantastic experience.

The Bon Shamans are not the only ones who consider the chakras to be tunnels. The Hopis of southwestern America as well as the Yaquis from the central plateau of Mexico share this belief.

To guide you, here is a glimpse of what these cultures affirm about the tunnels and the reservoirs of the chakras.

The first tunnel of power corresponds to the root chakra. This is the first place in a vast reservoir of genetic information, that contain all instinctive elements linked to survival in general, and to yours, in particular. We also find all ancestral information as well as the chronicle of all past lives. All this information becomes available in time when you become familiar with the first tunnel. Also note that to have access to this information, you must meet its guardian. We strongly suggest that you ask the help of your animal totem and your guide to facilitate this access.

When you visit the world of spirits by passing through this opening, you are first confronted with your fears. These often take the form of demons, giant insects, and nightmarish creatures straight out of horror films. You must confront them and recognize them for what they really are. That means the product of your imagination, the symbolic representation of what you are afraid of, your fears and your problems. Once you have faced them, you also learn to understand them and to conquer them. To overcome your fears does not always mean to fight with them, because very often, anger only nourishes them. Here again, your guides'help will be very useful. The goal of this exercise is to enable you to gain knowledge and to grow your personal power.

It is through this tunnel that you make your anchorage with the earth and everything that exists; that you can reinforce bonding with the planet.

The second tunnel of power corresponds to the genital organs chakra. This tunnel is intimately associated with the seat of brute emotions, with reproduction, fertility, sexuality, sexual attraction and sexual energy in general. All of the problems linked to one of these points can be diagnosed and dealt with at this tunnel's level.

When a Shaman travels through this tunnel, he must often face painful experiences the first times. He must often relive sexual aggression scenes that happened during his childhood and his adolescence and sometimes even during his adult life. Sometimes these scenes belong to past lives when one was either the aggressor or the victim. In addition, he may have to face his particular demons, his fears, what makes him afraid and his repressed desires. A voyage through this level is generally not very easy because we have all had traumatic experiences in our life. However, this enables the Shaman to overcome his fears and to heal his wounds.

One of the numerous advantages of working at this level is the growth of your own fertility as well as your creativity. All this new energy is very useful when you want to begin new projects and get rid of old ones that do not work.

The third tunnel of power corresponds to the solar plexus chakra. This tunnel is associated with action, affirmation, and visceral power. It also generates the vital energy that is indispensable to the life of the physical body. Some astral projection adepts use this center to leave and to enter into their physical bodies: these individuals describe their astral bodies to be connected to their physical bodies by a silver cord.

Experiences in this tunnel offer very useful personal perspectives for the Shaman. It is during these voyages that he can become aware of his habits and models that have governed his life until then. It is also at this place that he learns to acknowledge ideas and false concepts that he entertains about power. He also learns about the obstacles that he must overcome to use the power in question judiciously. Ferocious door-keepers like Cerberus guard these places. It is not easy to go through the doors that lead to these reservoirs of considerable power but they can help you to wait for success when the Shaman shows himself to be worthy.

The first level of easy accessible power is charisma, which becomes an indispensable trump card for the Shaman.

The other function of this tunnel is to act as an energy distributor for the physical body. This is a subtle function but the least unbalance is experienced as a feeling of tiredness and a lack of liveliness. It is essential to take into account the signs that can emit the third chakra, especially before taking on new tasks whether they be physical or spiritual.

The fourth tunnel of power corresponds to the heart chakra. This tunnel is associated with feelings: affection, intimacy, self-confidence and one's own affinity with the environment. This tunnel forms a bridge between the different levels of power like with the chakras.

It is also the seat for pardon. The faculty of pardoning others and oneself is fundamental for all satisfying Shamanic work. There probably exist other forms of Shamanism where pardon is an abstraction but we do not want to enter these paths.

When the Shaman voyages in this tunnel, he first feels all the sadness and all the grieving that he has ever known. This is an indispensable stage so that he can separate from all these sorrows and abandon them definitively. He sometimes has to relive or see certain scenes from past lives again because he did not know how to liberate himself from these actions.

This tunnel is probably the most used by the Shamans. After all, we must not forget that we need to love and be loved. We all need to be accepted and to have confidence in ourselves. This is also one of the reservoirs of energy that the Shaman can begin to easily perceive in others.

Let's experience this. When you meet someone good and generous, relax and let go. You will feel a current that comes from the heart chakra. It is the same thing when you meet someone who is suffering a lot. The energy quality changes but it comes from the same tunnel.

The information that you can draw from this reservoir is often linked to childhood memories. Unfortunately, you must confront the memories that are the most impacted such as feelings of abandonment, rejection, emotional frustrations and humiliation that create a lack of self-confidence. All the old disappointments are there and are waiting to be recognized. The Shaman must learn how to clean house and to pardon.

The fifth tunnel of power corresponds to the throat chakra. This tunnel is associated with communication, creative expression as well as the ability to channel. One of the consequences of using this tunnel frequently is to open our telepathic capacities, to receive and to understand messages coming from our guides as well as from our unconscious. If you want to become a medium, you must explore this tunnel in depth.

The first explorations of this passage open the door to all the unsaid words, all the repressed thoughts and all of the unexpressed emotions. Feelings of anger that have been buried for many years, often surface. You can end up with a sore throat and even lose your voice during the first experiences in this tunnel. You must also deal with your fears about not being able to express yourself correctly and the fear to be ridiculous.

The sixth tunnel of power corresponds to the third eye chakra. This tunnel represents the Shamanic capacity to see. This is the Shaman's vision. The ancient Egyptians represented this opening by a snake attached to a headband. The snake symbolized the faculty to see things spiritually.

When one uses this tunnel efficiently after long practice, it is possible for the Shaman to perceive individuals'illnesses which he can treat and diagnose correctly simply by looking at a patient.

One of the major obstacles to overcome while learning this tunnel is to recognize how you closed yourself in this vision in your childhood. The constantly evolving Shaman is confronted with events that caused this closure. At first glance this tunnel is dark and often full of shadows and fog. It is necessary to make light little by little to recover sight.

Patience is essential at the opening of this tunnel: headaches and even migraines may accompany efforts that are too quick.

The seventh tunnel of power corresponds to the crown chakra. For the Hopis, this tunnel is the opening through which the soul enters the physical body at birth and leaves at the moment of death. For the Yaquis, it is the entry and exit door for the Nagal, or astral body, that travels out of the physical body.

For other traditions, it is an anchor point with the cosmos where the energy of the universe can enter the body. It is also the entry door to esoteric and secret knowledge as well as wisdom and universal compassion that can go through all of the levels. ˙

Although many cultures use this tunnel for astral voyages, we do not recommend this. Ask the help of your animal totem or your guide before taking on such an experience.

The information reservoir at the level of this tunnel is difficult to access. Only a few individuals can understand the content and significance of the elements that are found here. This tunnel is an opening towards the superior level of spirituality.

How to reach tunnels of power

Here is a simple and efficient method to reach the different tunnels of power.

However, do not attempt to enter them without being accompanied by your guide or your totem animal. They know how to guide you and to explain how to proceed.

Relax completely by doing the nine breaths exercise.

- Think of the color of the chakra that corresponds to the tunnel that you intend to visit.

  Visualize this color and let yourself be impregnated by its energy. You can also recite the appropriate mantra.

- Once you have seen the color and have perceived the opening to the tunnel, ask for the presence of your guide before entering.

- Explain the reason of your visit and ask permission to explore the tunnel.

- Penetrate into the tunnel and carry out your exploration.

- Return to the opening.

- Thank your guide.

Chapter 6

The Teachings
of the Navajo People
and the Voodoo Tradition

❦⚊❦

The Navajo People

THE Navajo people, from the southwestern United States, are not originally from Arizona, where its members now live. This tribe was composed of warriors and was originally nomadic. After several centuries, the Hopi tribe asked the Navajo warriors for help against the invasion a neighboring tribe. The Navajos then settled in that region. They brought a very rich Shamanic tradition with them that holds a very different way of how to perceive individuals and how to communicate with them compared to all the other cultures. This perspective is particularly interesting for the Shaman because of the possibilities of communicating differently with others.

Three Types of Individuals;
Three Types of Communication

For the Navajo, there are three kinds of individuals who act in their own particular way in a given situation: those who respond with their head, those who respond with their heart and finally those who respond with their guts. To know which group someone belongs to and to be able to predict in which way he will respond is a very useful tool for the Shaman. He is able to determine in the wink of an eye how to communicate with this person, how to help her if she asks for help and how to negotiate if necessary. This knowledge increases the Shaman's power and helps him avoid errors on the journey by communicating with the different types of people. It is also a way to recognize what type of Shaman you are dealing with.

THE HEAD TYPE OF INDIVIDUALS

- **Directed**: by thoughts;
- **Their powers**: analysis, language, logic, philosophy, intuition;
- **Their deficiencies**: slow to respond, coldness, indifference, alienation.

These people's main tools are their brain and their vocal cords. They posses an extensive vocabulary and easily express themselves in general. They use language to assimilate their experiences and to communicate with others. Head individuals are orators and, often, writers who tend towards philosophy, analysis and logic. They tend to dissect an experience or event word by word, which allows them to analyze a problem in a systematic way and to find the root cause. These people easily conceptualize situations and generally understand what causes them. They work in scientific, research and business areas.

They are capable of explaining why they react in a certain way and the reasons why you should do the same. They prefer that ideas be presented in a linear and logical way. These people love to find answers, but it is almost impossible to satisfy them by an emotion or with a feeling. In these situations, they tend to consider these responses as hysterical or harmful. Head people do not have confidence in either emotions or feelings.

They prefer to logically analyze for a long time before moving or making any gestures. It is more interesting for them to think about the question than to directly reply. They have the gift of planning well, but concerning production... that's something else!

How to communicate with head individuals

- Let them speak first, which reassures them. However, do not let them draw out and get bogged down with extensive explanations.

- Try to get them to deviate from theory and lead them to the more practical.

- Be patient and do not move too quickly. You must not forget that these people think with words.

- When these head individuals have a problem, the last terrain they would chose would be the emotions. For example, when someone close dies, instead of grieving, they will study and analyze all of the ramifications of this event. They need someone else to bring them to their own emotions and to allow them to have disappointments; in short, to help them in such situations.

- Head individuals are proud of their talent for analysis, their ideas as well as their perspicacity, so remember to compliment them. They also need structure.

- These people are, however, very capable in remembering all of the Shamanic experiences that they undertake. Unfortunately, they lack emotional nuances; therefore, they also need help here.

- Head individuals need to thwart propensity by doing exercises and developing an interest in music.

THE INDIVIDUALS OF THE HEART

- **Directed:** by the emotions;

- **Their powers:** perception, speed, expression, inspiration;

- **Their deficiencies:** irrationality, subjectivity, and sentimentality.

These people put the accent on their heart and their lungs. Their head and the bottom of their body are put away on a shelf. For them, only emotions, feelings and inspiration exist. The rest doesn't count.

The heart individuals are very perspicacious, and they quickly evaluate a situation or a problem. They quickly perceive tension. For example, they can enter a room and feel when something is not going well without saying a word.

They instinctively know whom they can trust and who to avoid. Unfortunately, they cannot explain why. Their way of understanding is larger and less detailed than head individuals.

They operate according to a special matrix that defies analysis. The Shamans of the heart navigate between the past, the present and the future with ease, and they draw their information from all their sources before arriving at a conclusion. Unfortunately, they often forget to make a distinction between the three levels, which can cause them problems. Despite everything, they are often right in their analysis and their predictions, which make head people furious.

One of the biggest deficiencies of heart individuals is they are not capable of analyzing a situation unless they are directly involved. In other words, they lose themselves in their own feelings and emotions when considering problems.

They also have a tendency to constantly speak about their emotions and feelings even when they no longer feel them.

They consider head people to be robots and gut people as beings who react without thinking or without feeling anything.

Heart people can cause themselves problems because of their sentimentality or the subjectivity of their emotions. They sometimes mistake an emotion for a perception, which results in completely destroying their analysis.

They can also block access paths to their intellect and consequently, they are incapable of reasoning correctly. If they cut access to the gut path, because of overload, they lose the ability to react quickly and wallow in their emotions without accomplishing anything.

How to communicate with heart individuals.

- Let them express their feelings and emotions, even if this seems inappropriate. After a while it will be possible for them to listen to reason and to reach a larger objectivity by your asking them questions.

- Help them to concentrate their energy towards their legs or their abdomen. This will help them anchor their power at the root chakra level and the link with physical reality. The second chakra can also contribute to harmonize emotions and make them more manageable.

- Forget complicated plans and instructions. Heart individuals will rebel or be incapable of following them. If you have to work with them, make an exact schedule of repayment or delivery dates.

- Have confidence in their intuition. These individuals rarely make mistakes, even if that seems impossible to you.

- Use metaphors and parables to explain things to them. They are marvelous poets and artists. If possible, use images: an image is worth a thousand words and it is doubly true in their case.

- These people also have a tendency to dramatize their own Shamanic experiences, which leads to significant distortions. Ask them to simply describe what has happened.

- They are very sensitive and empathetic; unfortunately, they tend to identify with other people's problems and in this case, they are not efficient: they suffer more than the person who has the problem. Help them to take their distance concerning other people.

- To find balance, heart individuals must exercise and also focus intellectually on certain subjects.

THE INDIVIDUALS OF THE GUTS

- **Directed:** by action;
- **Their powers:** coordination, athletics, activity, instinct;
- **Their deficiencies:** impulsivity, frenzy, and automatisms.

The solar plexus region and lower limbs direct the gut individuals. Their credo is action and to produce a result. All of their emotions and feelings must be oriented towards action. Their ideas must also be linked to action.

They generally have exceptional coordination and athletic skills. They use their bodies in an instinctive way to understand how to use tools and machine instructions intuitively. They operate efficiently with bureaucracy.

They make the world move and experience much difficulty in doing nothing. They are happiest when going somewhere even in their heads. When they are unable to move physically, they easily imagine that they are somewhere else doing something or going somewhere. Their emotions also push them towards action.

These people use their heart to express their need of action often through dance or gestures. When they think, it is to arrange choreography or to build something. When they have an idea, they must immediately put it into practice. These people have no interest for philosophy, as all they want are results.

The danger that exists when they cut off from their head and their heart is that they become entirely mechanized and transform into a robot without a soul and react without thinking or feeling. Under such circumstances, gut individuals can fall into the trap of producing without a goal, without rationalizing or without perceiving the needs of others around them. Because of these tendencies, their personality can lead to alcoholic or drug dependency.

How to communicate with gut individuals

- These individuals need space. They are horrified to be in enclosed spaces where they feel closed in. Avoid confining them, as they prefer tasks that allow them to move.

- Give them opportunities to use their bodies, particularly if you are teaching them something. They really learn through action by repeating movements. To show them how to meditate, suggest rhythmic breathing, for example.

- The best compliment you can pay them is about their coordination.

- They have a memory of sensations and movement. Have them speak about these subjects first, then orient the conversation to emotions and to thoughts provoked by actions.

- They are generally impulsive, spontaneous and sometimes bellicose which teaches you a lot about their way of acting. You can also help them balance their emotions and their thought process.

- They can find balance in listening to music, by dancing and reading.

Sand paintings

Navajo Shamans practice this art. Their goal is to call in energies and have them converge on a precise point. Sand paintings are frequently used in healing ceremonies and can also serve other purposes.

They are not permanent. They serve to concentrate cosmic energy and, once they have served, they are simply erased. We know of this art form from the Navajos but they are not the only ones to use it. The Tibetans also use this form of Shamanic practice in certain peace and healing rituals.

As we are neither Navajo nor Tibetan Shamans, we cannot and should not try to recreate their paintings. However, we can use this technique to call in energy so that it concentrates on the subject that we hold dear to our heart.

SUPPLIES

- To make a sand painting, we naturally need different colored sand. You can easily buy this in large stores that sell sand for aquariums.

- You can also collect sand from beaches or create your own sand from table salt that you can color with food coloring.

Rituals to create paintings

To attract peace into your home:

- This ritual is particularly beneficial if incidents such as quarrels, robbery etc. have happened in your space. The aim of this painting is to assure calm in your home.

- You will need **white**, **blue** and **purple** sand.

- You should create your painting on the floor of your house or on a big table if you have a rug.

- The day before the ritual, clean the surface that will receive the painting thoroughly. When that is finished, place your bowls of sand here and leave them there over night.

- The next day after a bath or a shower to purify yourself, dress in comfortable natural fiber clothes.

- Kneel near the surface where you intend to create your painting, if it is on the floor.

- Take some white sand in your more powerful hand (the one you write with). Concentrate for a few minutes.

- Let a thin stream of sand flow and draw the form of your house, apartment or the place where you live. While doing this, repeat these words: *Here is my house!* Add as much sand as necessary to draw your house the best you can.

- Then take some blue sand and draw a circle around your house by going clockwise without touching the drawing of your house but by completely surrounding it. While doing this, repeat these words: *Here is my house!*

- Then take the purple sand and trace a circle around the blue circle clockwise. This time the circles touch: surround the blue circle and your house.

- Repeat these words: *Here is my house bathing in a circle of serenity and peace.*

- Now concentrate on the image that you have created by calling cosmic energy to consecrate your ritual. Imagine blue and purple energy that now surround your house. Feel the energy vibrate around you. Meditate on the subject for a few minutes.

- Then sweep the sand, knowing that your ritual has worked.

- You can keep your sand or throw it in the toilet but do not use it for another ritual.

TO HELP BRING ABOUT HEALING

You will need blue, white, yellow, red and purple sand.

- You can use this ritual for yourself or for another person, who does not have to be present. Call in the energies and you can direct them anywhere.

- Take some blue sand and trace a square of about sixty centimeters (two feet) by repeating these words: *Here is healing energy.*

- Take some white sand and trace the form of a body in the middle of the square (you can make a stick man if you cannot draw very well, as this is only a symbolic representation). Make it big enough so you can put sand inside and say these words: *Here is the body of..., who is ill, where the energy does not circulate very well.*

- Now take some yellow sand and place a little inside the form of the head of this personage by saying: *Here is the mind of..., it now works perfectly and he is liberated of all negative thought.*

- Now take some red sand and place it at the heart level of your personage by saying: *Here is the heart of..., it now works perfectly and is filled with love and is free of all guilt and is able to pardon others and himself.*

- Now take some purple sand and create an aura around your personage. The form will perfectly match the last one. Move it clockwise and repeat: *Here is the soul of..., in perfect harmony with body and mind.*

Now transform the blue square that surrounds your painting with a circle with your dominant hand. Begin with the right corner. By working slowly and with care, round the corner until it takes the form of a circle. Feel the energy concentrate in all parts of your painting.

- When your square has become a circle, say:

  Here is the healed body of..., *where energy circulates perfectly.*

  His thoughts are free and positive.

  His love is strong and free from guilt.

  His soul is in perfect harmony with his thoughts and his body.

  Healing energy enters freely in... and now materializes.

- Concentrate for a few minutes on healing energy by directing it towards the person in question. Visualize the energy penetrating him.

- When this is finished, sweep the sand and throw it in the toilet. You can also put it in a glass pot and give it to the person concerned.

As you can see, the principle is relatively simple. You trace a representation of what you wish and you use different colored sand to symbolize the transformation of what you want to do.

COLORS AND THEIR PROPERTIES

White
- Favors protection and purification. This is the basic color to represent people or objects in your paintings.

Blue
- Symbolizes healing, peace, the psyche, patience and happiness.

Brown
- Symbolizes animals and land acquisition.

Yellow
- Favors intellect, confidence, divination and communication; facilitates movements and travel.

Black
- Serves to banish the negative and absorbs unbeneficial energies. This color allows you to create a vortex to get rid of negative influences and harmful spells.

Orange
- Increases all types of energies and is also the color that facilitates attraction.

Pink
- Represents love, friendship, compassion and relaxation. This color symbolizes the most tender emotions and noble sentiments.

Red

- Enables to recover or to maintain health and enhance physical strength and energy. Augments courage and protection. It is also the color of passion.

Green

- Represents prosperity, money, work, fertility, healing and growth.

Purple

- Serves to enhance Shamanic power and to heal serious illness; represents spirituality and meditation.

Voodoo

Voodoo is probably the Shamanic tradition that has been most written about yet is the least known. It is one of the most recent traditions from a historical point of view, although its roots are very ancient. When one thinks of voodoo, one often imagines the world of zombies, snakes and the jungle. We think of drum rhythms, rum that flows in streams and curses with bewitched dolls.

Where does voodoo really come from? It first saw the light of day on plantations on islands like Haiti and in Louisiana, especially in New Orleans with the slaves who came from Africa. To understand its origin, as we know the majority of the slaves came from Nigeria, particularly the Yoroubas tribes that were composed of numerous clans who fought with each other. The vanquished were sold to the slave traders who were often Arabs who worked for French slave ships.

The slaves crossed the ocean under deplorable conditions: more than a third died before arriving at their destination. The original culture of these people was very primitive but very rich in Shamanic rituals. Upon their arrival, the slaves paid homage to their gods for allowing them to survive. However, they had to endure the white man's tyranny and embrace his religion or be beaten.

This is when voodoo was born because the survivors of the long voyage at sea continued to honor their deities. However, they took into account that the white man had even more powerful allies than theirs because they had been enslaved.

This is why those people who remembered the ancient African practices juxtaposed the African gods with the Catholic pantheon of saints. The concept of only one god was a little preposterous for these beings; the juxtaposition between the saints and the deities of the Yorouba cult happened quite quickly. The slaves used one stone for two hits. Firstly, they adhered to the new religion of the white man and, secondly, they also continued to honor their own gods that were prohibited to them.

To give you an example, Yemanja, the goddess of water, became the other face of the Virgin Mary. Papa Legba became connected to Saint Antoine and so on. This cult found several different forms. In Brazil, it was named le candomble. In Mexico it was the santeria (which literally means "the cult of the saints"). The practice of voodoo, under different forms, is very well known now and despite the bad reputation created in Hollywood and the media, it is a true religion and not a black magic practice.

Voodoo dolls

The principle of the voodoo doll or effigy is relatively simple. It concerns a magic practice of similarity.

The doll or effigy represents the person on whom you want to work.

This is not about planting needles to harm but rather to transform the energy and to actualize it in the physical world.

The Shamanic practices are not good or bad in themselves, as it is always a question of intention.

If you work for the good, then you will harvest. If you work for the bad, you should be ready to assume the consequences of your acts.

HOW TO CONSTRUCT AN EFFIGY

The method that we recommend is from New Orleans. It is simple to do and gives rather spectacular results.

To do it, find two sticks to form a cross. This is one of the most powerful symbols that exists.

- Form the body and the limbs of the doll at the long part of the cross, so that the cross part represents the arms.

Cover the top of the stick with moss that you can find in nature or at a florist's shop.

- Form a ball and cover it with white cloth for the head.

- Close the neck with a cord or thread.

- Then take a piece of cloth of the appropriate color (see the list on pages 200 and 201) and make a robe or a sack that you can fill with the moss to form the body of your doll.

- The results do not have to be artistic: it is a symbol, a representation of the person who you are treating or who wants to obtain something.

When your doll is ready, procure some hair and nail cuttings from the person that you put into the doll's body.

- When these elements are in place, this effigy becomes a representation of the person because it contains a physical part of the being in question. You are now ready to cast a spell on the effigy.

Burn your favorite incense.

- Light a candle of the same color as the doll's robe.

Recite the following invocation while passing and re-passing the effigy in the incense smoke:

- *Papa Legba. Papa Legba. Open the door to hidden knowledge so that I can obtain my wish.*

  This effigy is a representation of...

  Let this person receive... (healing, money, work, etc.)

  I pray to you, Papa Lega, to act in my favor.

  I pray that all powers come to help me.

  My intentions are pure and my need is great.

  Intercede for me so that I can obtain my wish.

Your desire to help yourself or to help another person is the vehicle that allows your wish to be granted.

The energy circulates where attention and concentration are located.

As you have noticed, this practice is very simple and you can use it as you wish.

You can use effigies for a multitude of possibilities.

All desires and all rituals are possible with the dolls.

Here is a list of the appropriate colors for the candles and robes for the effigies or the dolls.

Silver
- All the spells that neutralize negativity encourage stability and attract the influence of the goddesses.

White
- All the consecration and dedication spells; those that deal with divination, exorcism, clairvoyance, healing as well as those that favor peace, truth, spirituality and lunar energy.

Blue
- All the spells that touch on honor, loyalty, peace, tranquility, truth, wisdom, sleep protection, astral projection and prophetic dreams.

Brown
- All the spells for finding lost objects; to ameliorate your power of concentration, to increase your telepathic powers and to protect domestic animals.

Grey
- All the spells that serve to neutralize negative or unbeneficial influences.

Yellow
- All the spells of attraction, of charm and of persuasion as well as those that increase self-confidence.

Black
- All the spells that implicate meditation, to thwart evil curses or maledictions, to unknot negative spells, to get rid of negative and harmful influences, to banish negative energies as well as evil spirits.

Gold
- All of the spells that attract the powers of cosmic influences and honor solar deities.

Orange
- All the spells that stimulate energy and sexuality.

Pink
- All the spells that concern friendship and all the aspects of femininity.

Red
- All the spells concerning fertility, aphrodisiacs, those that stimulate passion, love, health, physical strength, vengeance, the will, courage and magnetism.

Green
- All the spells that include fertility, success, luck, prosperity and ambition as well as those that neutralize degeneration, avarice and jealousy.

Purple
- All the spells that involve psychic manifestations, healing as well as those that involve power, independence and protection of your home.

Here is now a small guide that will give you an idea about the appropriate spells, the colors and the incense for each day of the week.

SUNDAY
- Spells for exorcism, healing and to attract prosperity;

Colors
- Orange, white and yellow;

Incense
- Lemon and oliban.

MONDAY
- Spells for feminine fertility, reconciliation, for those who take care of agriculture, animals, messages and voyages;

Colors
- Silver, white and grey;

Incense
- Violet, honeysuckle, willow, and absinthe.

TUESDAY
- Spells for vengeance, to break an evil spell and maledictions; those that augment courage, physical strength and surgical operations;

Colors
- Red and orange;

Incense
- Dragon blood and patchouli.

WEDNESDAY

- Spells for communication and divination; to augment the gifts of writing, divination and knowledge;

Colors

- Yellow, grey and mauve;

Incense

- Jasmine, lavender and sweet pea.

THURSDAY

- To attract luck, happiness, health, treasures and riches; to resolve legal problems, to augment masculine fertility;

Colors

- Blue, indigo and purple;

Incense

- Cinnamon, musk, nutmeg and sage.

FRIDAY

- To attract love, marriage, romance, partners; to augment physical beauty, to sort out problems of a sexual nature;

Colors

- Pink, green, turquoise and chartreuse;

Incense

- Vanilla, strawberry, sandalwood and rose.

SATURDAY

- To communicate with the spirits, to combat psychic attacks; to overcome enemies, to help meditation as well as to find lost objects and people who have disappeared;

Colors

- Black, grey and indigo;

Incense

- Poppy seed and myrrh.

Conclusion

E have just been through a short tour of the Shamanic universe. We hope this guide will be useful for your spiritual quest. As you have seen by reading the preceding pages, Shamanism is still practiced today and continually transforms to adapt to our urban lives, that still have many common points with the traditional environments of long ago.

Shamanic practice is perfect for our present times because it is tolerant and uses the best of all worlds. We invite you to follow this path and to innovate.

The Shamanic world is enriched with each new practice that you invent. Do not hesitate to reformulate the invocations, to re-write the meditation texts or to adapt the practices. In doing this, you become a Shaman in the purest tradition. Remember: there is always another way of going about doing things!

Bibliography

ANDERSON, Joseph L. The Wisdom of the Serpent,
Collier Books.

BECKLEY, Timothy Green. Kahuna Powers,
Inner Light.

BIERHORST, John. The Mythology
of North American Indians.

CASTANEDA, Carlos. A Yaqui Way of Knowledge,
Simon & Schuster.

ELIADE, Mircea. Le sacré et le profane,
Collection Idées.

ERDOES, Richard. American Indian Shamanism,
Healing Arts Press.

HOFFMAN, Albert. Shamanic Rituals, Healing Arts Press.

KAHILI KING, Serge. Urban Shaman, Simon & Schuster.

LELAND, Charles G. Aradia, Phoenix Press.

MacCROSSAN, Tadhg. The Truth About the Druids, Llewellyn.

MILLMAN, Dan. Peaceful Warrior.

OSUMI, Ikuko. The Shamanic Healer, Healing Arts Press
Quill-William Morrow.

SAINT-CLAIR, D. Drum & Candles, DoubleDay.

STEVENS, Jose. Secrets of Shamanism, Avon New Age.

VAUCH, Aba. Magie tibétaine, Éditions Savoir pour Être.

Contents